Beat it!

Serious drum patterns from Heavenly Music's
Joe and Pauly Ortiz

Beat it!

Serious drum patterns from Heavenly Music's
Joe and Pauly Ortiz

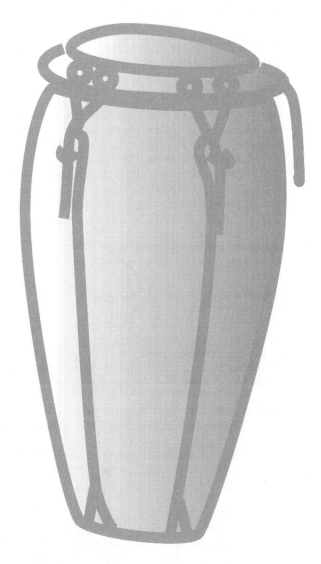

PC Publishing

PC Publishing
Export House
130 Vale Road
Kent TN9 1SP
UK

Tel 01732 770893
Fax 01732 770268
email pcp@cix.compulink.co.uk
web site http://www.pc-pubs.demon.co.uk

First published 1997

© Heavenly Music MIDI Software

ISBN 1 870775 46 5

British Library Cataloguing in Publication Data
A catalogue record for this book is available from the British Library

Printed by Bell & Bain Ltd., Glasgow

Software licence agreement
This data must not be used to print musical notation. The manufacture of
sheet music derived from this data is strictly prohibited

Conditions of use
The patterns on the accompanying disk may be used for user's demos,
rehearsals, live performance, etc. The user may incorporate the patterns into
a commercial audio recording provided that credits appear on packaging
and/or labels in the form of: *Additional rhythm programming by Heavenly
Music MIDI Software.*

Disclaimer
No liability will be accepted by Heavenly Music MIDI Software for
consequential loss or damage however caused arising as a result of using our
software. No guarantees can be given that the data will perform on
subsequent MIDI equipment. This disk and all data contained are guaranteed
for a period of one year from date of purchase against faults not arising
from any mis-use, neglect or accidental erasure caused by the end user.

Contents

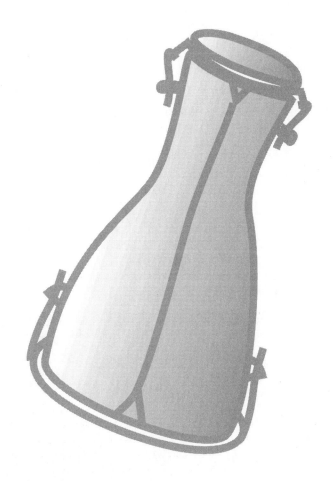

Dedication

For Evy May Moore 1922–1996, with all our love.

About the authors

Joe and Pauly Ortiz are Heavenly Music (alias *Heaven on Earth*). A partnership that has dedicated a couple of lifetimes to *music*. They are writers, arrangers, producers, engineers, programmers, instrumentalists and vocalists (to name but a few of their nicer points).

Heavenly Music was formed in England in 1988 as a front end to deal with Virgin Music and Atlantic Records in the US, as that is who they were writing and making records for at the time under the name of 'Heaven On Earth'. Their single *On An Angels Wing* (a soul record) became pick of the week on London's Capital Radio, and to this day continues to be played worldwide.

Software to their credit includes (Dr.Beat, The Jam Files, Mega Trax MIDI Song Files and the BCK SMF Series. Their TV music credits include the theme from the antiques program *Heirlooms*, the wildlife theme for *Animals In Action* and the music for the ITV game show *Jumble*. Their original compositions can also be heard demonstrating some of the latest hi tech MIDI music equipment on the market.

Pauly Ortiz began music aged 4, and is the voice, keyboardist and co-writer of the above mentioned LP and single. Her first LP release (*Ladies Fire*) saw the issue of two singles *One Of The Chosen Few* and *Jimmy's Hi Fi* on CBS Records Europe. These singles became instant turntable hits with the likes of Dave Lee Travis on BBC Radio 1. With a voice reminiscent of Aretha Franklin, Pauly also composes and sequences her own tracks.

Joe Ortiz has been performing since age 5 and is ex studio and touring lead guitarist for *Inner Circle* . He has played live and sessioned in New York, Nassau and London with the likes of Steve Gadd, Anthony Jackson, Hugh Masekela, Dave Grusin, Steve Ferrone, Ian Dury, Ruben Blades, Dave Valentin, Pino Paladino and more. A multi-instrumentalist, he also plays bass, drums and percussion and keyboards.

They have a 12 year old son, Paul, who has been contributing his part to the programming team since age 6!

Count in

Drummers have to be some of the most complicated people on the planet – but then so would you be if you had to split your brain into six bits to deal with four independent limbs, a pair of ears and, if you're sight reading, your eyes. It would be an absolute nightmare if you're one of those people who have a problem walking and sipping a drink through a straw at the same time. Drummers are special though – not least, because, under the control of a competent drummer that knows his or her instrument, the four independent limbs referred to above are in absolute harmony. You only need to listen to a track like Santana's *Head, Hands and Feet* (see Chapter 8) featuring Graham Lear, or Simon Phillips on Jeff Beck's *Space Boogie* to experience the masters at work.

Almost everyone at some point looks at a drum kit and wonders what it would be like just to give it a bash. Although I am a guitarist, I have to admit to being a closet drummer, and whenever the opportunity is presented, I will have a bash. We make it a point to keep a wide open menu of musical styles and musicians – sax players, bass players, keyboard players – and *drummers*. We've also been fortunate enough to have done session work with guys like Steve Gadd, Steve Ferrone, Arron Ahmun, Calvin Mc Kenzy, and others – giving us as close a look as we could get – at what makes a great drummer groove.

My star pupils in rhythm programming (Pauly and young Paul Ortiz) are testament to how good drum and percussion programming is possible without resorting to MIDI drum pads, as some of the following patterns were played in by them.

This book is designed to help you learn how to play (on a real kit) or, if you use a hard or software MIDI setup, program your own realistic drum and percussion patterns. Not only can you read about a pattern, or see it in a grid – but through the use of MIDI files as presented on the disk – you can hear what you're reading about. If you use a MIDI sequencer and know how to access its edit facilities, you can gain even more detailed knowledge about phrasing, dynamics and so on. No more eight armed octopus drummers either.

Styles are grouped into the following: 50s, 60s and Pop, Dance and Soul, Jazz and World Rhythms which might include patterns like Reggae, Soca, Calypso, Jazz and Latin (these styles continue to influence mainstream Rock, Soul, Dance and other music in a big way), and finally Rock and R&B.

Grid format

The patterns are presented in a grid format with the top of the grid horizontally representing bars and beats while the left vertical column is used to identify the separate elements of the drum and percussion line-up. You will probably have seen grids like this, especially if you followed the series on groove programming which we wrote for *Sound On Sound* magazine.

A lot of rhythm programming books have used this grid system to illustrate a pattern, so if you've read similar books you'll feel right at home. Note that the rhombs (diamond shapes representing the actual beats) in the grid illustrations are coloured according to velocity, the darker ones indicating the higher velocity values.

Variations

Most of the files on the accompanying disk are illustrated by more than one diagram. This is because there can be one, two or more variations on a given style. In some instances, fills or end rolls may also be illustrated.

Playing style

Another difference you'll find in this book is that individual drums may be referred to by what part of a drummer's body is striking them – i.e. the right hand on the hi hat or the right foot on the kick or bass drum (assuming you're a right handed drummer). If you're a keyboard player, in the long run, it might be a good idea to start seeing your fingers as other parts of your body. According to the current GM (General MIDI) specification, you'll have two bass drums to play with – namely B0 and C1 – so strengthen up that middle finger on your left hand cause that's the drummer's right foot and needs a lot of kick. Your left hand index finger or thumb can be the drummer's left hand for playing snare (D1 and E1), rim shots (C#1) and the occasional hi hat during a fill.

Your right hand index finger will be the drummer's right arm for hi hats, crash and ride cymbals and, in combination with your left hand index finger, fills and rolls on the kit's toms.

Techie bits
A full drum note assignment map is included at the end of this book for your reference, as well as a list of MIDI controllers which can be used to add even more variety and expression.

The files on disk can of course be used to rehearse or jam along with. You can also try importing them into your own demo songs – they can make an instant difference. If any of the files should be used for commercial purposes, please see 'conditions on use' at the beginning of the book, and while you're at it, send us a copy – we love to hear what our users get up to.

Happy programming (and beating)!

Note: When referring to beat elements of a phrase, the American names are used, i.e. whole, half, quarters, eighths, sixteenths and so on. We hope that this will be more of a help than a hindrance to your understanding of rhythm.

Triplet eighth ballad (8TBALLD1)

This pattern uses the ride as a simple accent for the beginning. The hi hats play triplet eighths as described earlier. Finally, the snare is used on beats 2 and 4 of each bar with the exceptions of fills. A tambourine on beats 2 and 4 of each bar is used to enhance the snare beats, and this could be particularly effective during intros, chorus, middle eights and endings.

Variation

This pattern introduces a few upbeats on the snare with build up on the snare and open hi hat out of the pattern into the next.

Triplet eighth mid tempo (8TMIDTEM)

This pattern features the right hand playing triplet eighths but missing the second triplet eighth on the hi hat and, later, the ride cymbal.

The left hand plays the snare every second and fourth beat of the bar, while the right foot plays on a single then double pattern based around the same triplet eighths. Occasionally, the bass drum will throw in the odd up-beat triplet just before the next bar begins.

Variation 1

As in triplet eighth ballad, this variation uses a build up which makes a nice lead in to either another verse or chorus section. The tambourine on beats 2 and 4 helps to accent the snare beats. You can try using the tambourine on just beat 4 of each bar for verses.

Variation 2

This is identical to the basic pattern except that the ride is used instead of the hi hat. This pattern works well in a middle eight or solo section of a song.

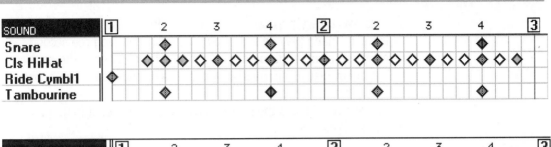

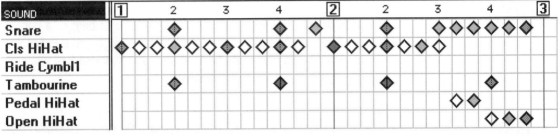

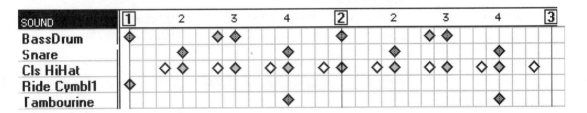

Late sixties (LATE60S)

This was a very popular style of drumming in the 60s and features the right hand playing triplet eighths again, missing the second eighth as also happens when playing the ride. Later in the pattern, the hi hat plays solid quarter notes on a splashy half open hi hat.

The left hand plays the snare on every quarter building up to a triplet eighth fill.

The bass drum skips along always playing the first beat of a bar, but judicious use of up-beat triplet eighths through the middles and beginnings of a bar give this pattern a very light loose feel while still managing to retain an excitement.

Variation 1
This pattern uses a basic but effective snare fill on every triplet eighth beat as a lead up to a chorus section.

Variation 2
Identical to the basic pattern, the hi hat is replaced by a light airy ride cymbal. This pattern is good for a chorus or middle eight section of a song.

Loose triplet eighths (LOOSE8T)

This pattern is a bit of a weird one in that it is not rigidly tied to exact triplet eighths. It's almost as if it's fighting to be a straight eighth pattern. This is apparent in the hi hat and bass drum patterns. Notice again, the missing second triplet hi hat beat.

Variation
Same as the basic pattern except that it uses some light snare strokes on the upbeats to beats 2 and 4 and so serves well as a fill pattern. You can probably get through a whole song in this style using just these two patterns!

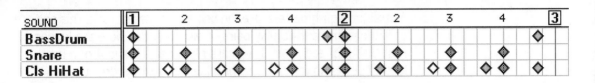

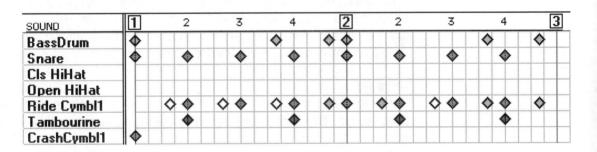

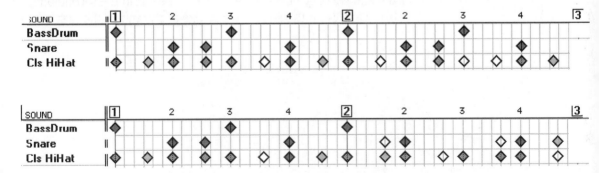

Mid tempo 1 (MIDTEMP1)

A straight eighth pattern used in so many styles of rock, this one uses the right hand to play pairs of eighth notes. Note the louder first eighth of each pair. The snare plays beats 3 and 4 of a bar loosely deviating from this to provide eighths or sixteenths for minor fills.

This pattern, although used a lot in the 60s still makes its way into the charts. Slowed down, it can be used for a soul ballad or, speeded up, a nice mid tempo pop track.

Variation 1
This uses an open splashy hi hat to add excitement to the pattern which makes a good chorus or middle eight section. Note that although it is an eighth beat pattern, sixteenth beat fills may still be used as in the ending of this variation on the snare part.

Intro fill
Notice the ramp in velocity on the snare drum as it cracks into the intro section. This intro fill is still widely used as an intro to a rock track.

Variation 2
This pattern contains a powerful off beat accent using the bass drum and crash cymbal on the upbeat of beat 2 in the second and fourth bars. Note the light snare stroke at the end of the first bar.

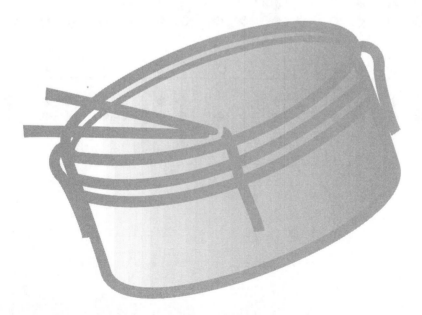

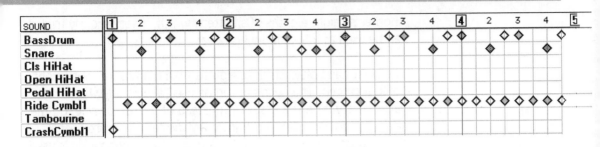

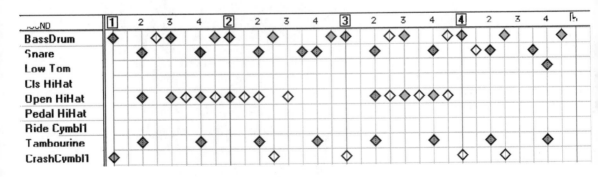

Mid tempo 2 (MIDTEMP2)

Another straight eighths 60s pattern which, if very slightly tripled, can be used as a Soul II Soul groove!

The right hand plays straight eighths with the first of every eight being accented. The open hat can be used almost anywhere for variety – try it on the first beat (instead of a crash or ride, or, the second or fourth beat (not third). Try the eighth before beat 2 and/or 4 or even every second eighth in a bar. Tambourine is used to accent the snare beats 2 and 4. Note that the left hand playing snare plays a sixteenth up-beat before each third beat of the bar. This provides the looseness of this pattern.

The right foot always plays the first beat of the bar, although you can try pushing this back or forward an eighth or sixteenth for more variety.

Variation 1
Almost identical to the basic pattern except that it uses a crash at the start of each bar.

Variation 2
Same as the basic pattern but using the ride cymbal instead of the hi hat.

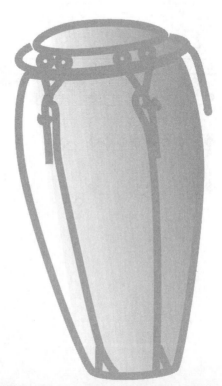

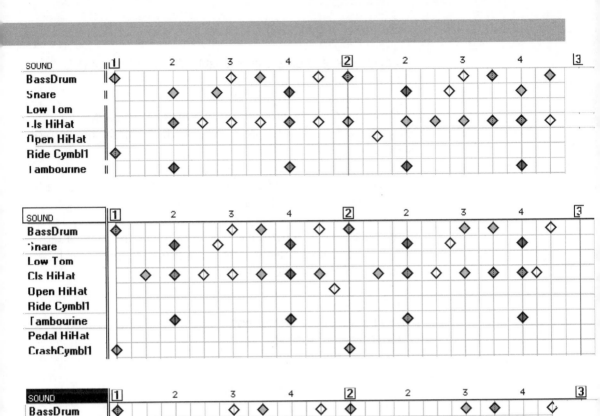

Phil Spector 1(P_SPECT1)

As the filename implies, this is a pattern used in a lot of Phil
Spector records.

A straight eighth pattern, this one features a solid bass drum
(always playing the first beat in a bar) with an eighth note up-beat
before beat 3 of a bar.

The toms are used for fills in quarter note triplets while the crash
is used almost every eight bars or measures.

The real spice in this pattern comes from the tambourine pattern
which starts out as straight eighths but deviates on the fourth beat
to rattle in 32nds or 32nd triplets.

Fill 1
This fill uses triplet quarter notes on the snare and mounted tom at
the third beat of the bar.

Fill 2
Same as fill 1 but using the snare and mounted toms.

Phil Spector 2(P_SPECT2)

Another much used Spector feel. This one features tambourine
playing sixteenths, always accenting the first sixteenth of each beat
and adding an urgency to the pattern.

The right hand is playing a very loose eighths hi hat pattern
(accenting the first of every pair of eighths) while the left hand
plays every second and fourth beats in the bar.

Bass drum always plays the first beat in a bar adding an up-beat
eighth before beat 3 of a bar. The crash cymbal can grace the first
beat of every eight or sixteen bars.

Variation 1
Here, the pattern breaks down to a mere bass and snare drum.
This pattern makes for a good verse section or as a lead up to the
end of a song.

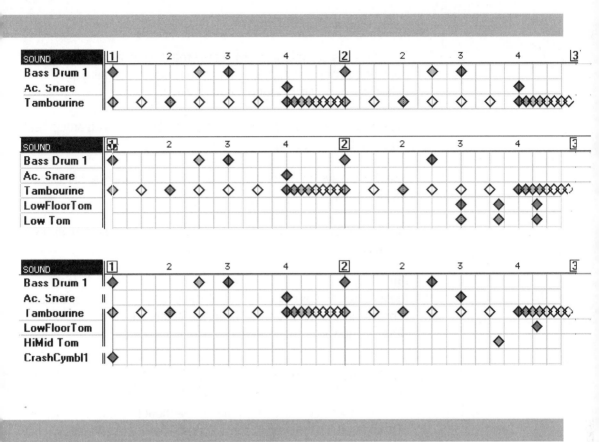

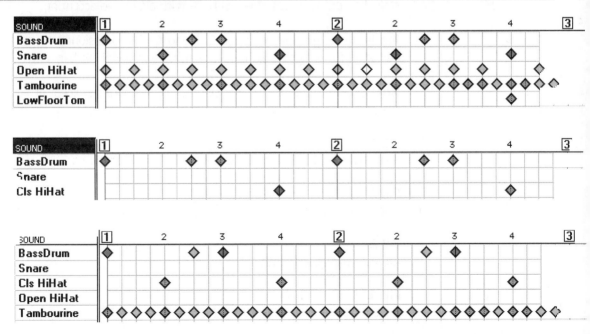

Quick shuffle (QUIKSHUF)

This pattern uses the hi hat to supply the drive in eighth notes accenting every first eighth of a pair, but notice a slight gap between every pair of eighths – almost triplet again.

Bass drum always plays on the first beat of the bar with an up-beat eighth note before beat 3 of the bar.

The snare plays on beats 2 and 4 of the bar deviating at bar 8 for a sixteenth fill.

To round it off, the claps are used on every second and fourth beat in the bar.

Fill
Identical to the basic pattern but at the upbeat of beat 3 of the bar, it breaks into sixteenth snare beats to fill into the next bar.
Note the upward ramping velocity of the snare fill.

Rock n roll 1 (ROKROLO1)

This one goes back further to the 50s, although it was used in the 60s and is still used now in some songs. The right hand plays straight eighths on the ride cymbal – with almost no accenting.

The left hand plays snare on beats 2 and 4 while occasionally deviating for either an eighth, sixteenth, or wilder fill at bar 4 or 8.

Note There is practically no bass drum in this pattern except at the start of a bar after a fill.

Fill 1
This sixteenth fill begins at the upbeat of beat 3 of the bar.

Fill 2
Triplet sixteenths start rolling again, at the upbeat of 3.

Fill 3
Another triplet sixteenth snare drum fill.

Fill 4
A plain vanilla flavoured sixteenth snare fill.

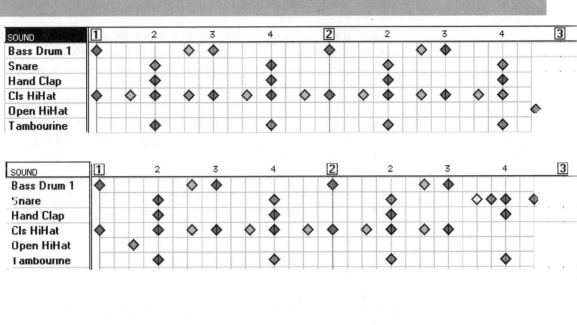

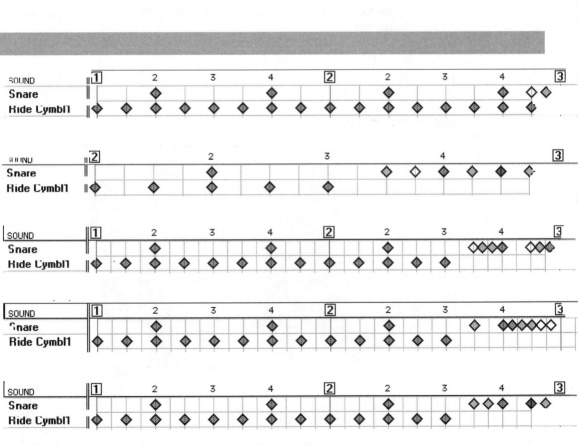

Dance/soul 1 (BARRIERS)

One of the many flavours available in current dance music, this pattern features the bass drum playing every *quarter* note of the bar while both hands are busy playing the sixteenth hi hat pattern. Claps are used to at least emphasise beats 2 and 4 of the bar.

Bongos and conga are used to help this pattern along with the open low conga playing every up-beat eighth before each fourth and first beats of the bar.

Stopping and starting at seemingly arbitrary points in a song also seem to be the norm with this type of music.

Intro
Same as the basic but without the bass drum.

Variation
China cymbals crashing on beats 1 and 2 of each bar lend some excitement to this variation pushed along by choppy sixteenth go go bells.

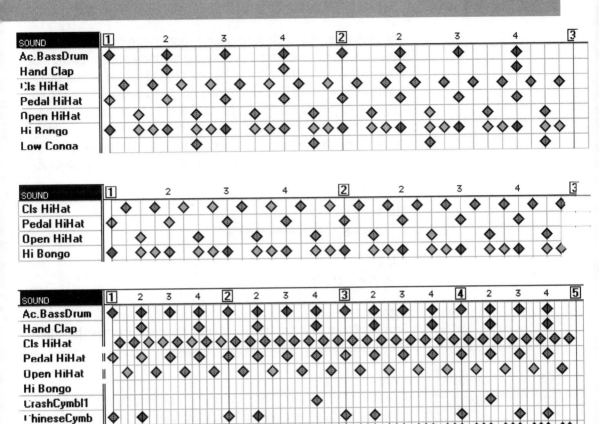

Dance/soul 2 (BLOWITUP)

The bass drum plays straight quarter notes with no variation in dynamics. Both hands are busy playing a sixteenth beat pattern on the hi hat (raising the left foot to open the hi hat on the up-beat eighth of every beat) although the right hand is taken away from this task to play the snare on beats 2 and 4 of the bar while the left hand is taken away to play the up-beat sixteenth snare beat before every third beat of the bar. To really make this pattern move, a sixteenth cabasa pattern is used. Claps also play beats 2 and 4.

Fill 1
A broken sixteenth beat snare fill.

Fill 2
A simple snare fill.

Intro 1
Straight fours (quarter note beats) on the bass drum with pedal and closed hi hats playing sixteenth beats.

Intro 2
As in the basic pattern, the bass drum is playing straight quarter note beats while the closed hi hats play sixteenths with an open hat on every third sixteenth.

Note In most current dance music, it seems acceptable to use an eight armed drummer, as demonstrated by this pattern.

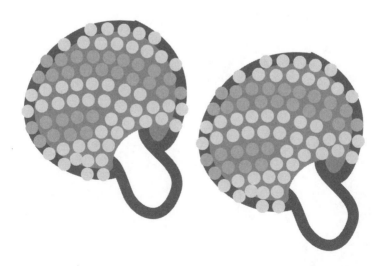

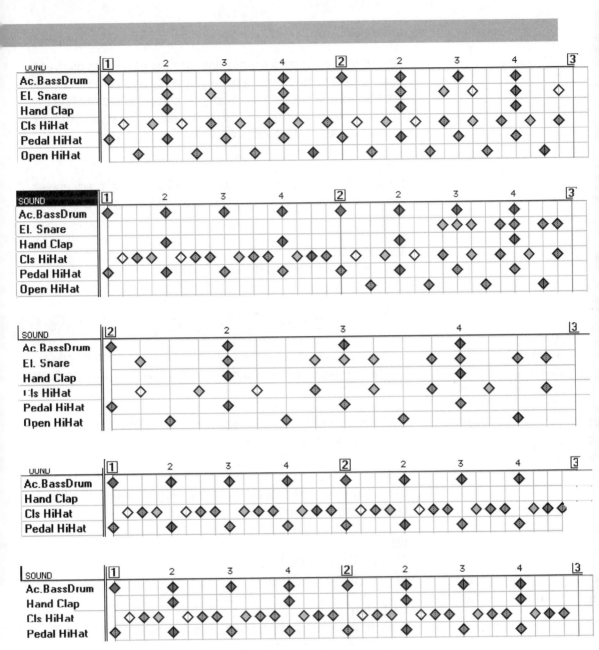

Dance/soul 3 (CANTFEEL)

Similar to the last pattern, this one uses the bass drum on every quarter note while the right hand plays on every up-beat of every quarter note. A sixteenths tambourine pattern is accented on every quarter note and is used to add movement to the style. Claps are used to accent beats 2 and 4 of the bar.

Intro
Straight four bass drum with the closed hat playing every upbeat eighth while the tambourine plays sixteenths accented every first sixteenth.

Variation
Same as basic pattern without the bass drum and claps.

Dance/soul 4 (DANCE1)

This pattern sounds as if there are two different patterns playing at the same time! The bass drum generally provides a straight quarter note pattern but then breaks into sixteenths missing every second sixteenth in the beat – wild. Claps are played on beats 2 and 4 while the right hand plays eighth note hi hats. The left foot opens the hat on every up-beat eighth of beats 3 and 4.

Fill
Not really a fill – but a space for some sampled speech or other noise to help bring in the song.

Intro
Straight fours on the bass drum with closed hat on beats 2 and 4 of every bar of the intro.

Variation
Straight fours on bass drum with snare on beat two and sixteenth upbeat snare after beat 4 in the bar.

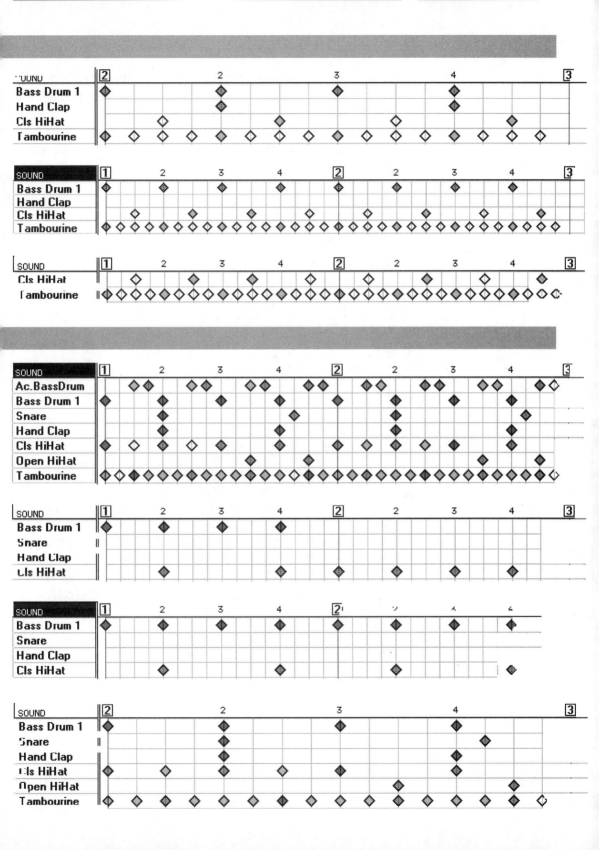

Dance/soul 5 (DANCEY)

Tambourine features heavily in playing a sixteenth pattern (missing every second sixteenth of the bar) while the bass drum plays solidly on every quarter note of the bar. The left hand plays the snare on every second and fourth beat with an occasional up-beat sixteenth thrown in just before beat 3 of the bar. The right hand is playing a copy of the tambourine pattern.

Intro
Tambourine playing broken sixteenths i.e. the second sixteenth is left out in each bar. The closed hat plays upbeat eighths.

Variation
Same as basic but using a crash at the start of the bar.

Dance/soul 6 (DANGLING)

Bass drum always plays the first beat of the bar with an up-beat before every third beat in the bar. Snare and claps play every second and fourth beats of the bar while the hi hat plays what you might call a randomly broken sixteenth beat pattern. Notice the sparse use of latin percussion in this pattern which provides loads of space for the rest of the 'band'. The seemingly echoed cabasa pattern is created by playing triplet eighths – then ramping the velocity from loud to soft.

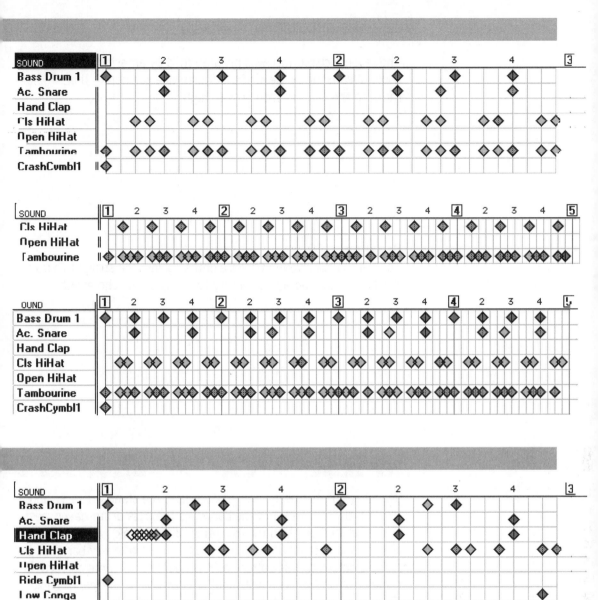

Dance/soul 6 (DANGLING) – continued

The reverse clap effect was programmed by entering sixteenth triplets from the up-beat of the fourth quarter note – then ramping the velocity from low to high.

Variation
The Cabasa is played in triplet eighths against the straight fours of this beat with a decaying velocity to simulate an echo effect.

Dance/soul 7 (IKNOWHY)

Swingbeat at its finest – this pattern uses the standard snare and claps on beats 2 and 4 of the bar while the bass drum *never* sees beat 1 of the bar (with the exception of the break). A sixteenth tambourine pattern accented on the first beat of every bar adds the swing element to this pattern as it is quantised or time corrected to somewhere in-between a straight sixteenth and a sixteenth triplet. The open high conga is playing only from the up-beat sixteenth before bar 3 and out again before beat 4 of the bar and is quantised or time corrected to the same values used for the tambourine.

Main pattern
As above but introduces the snare on beats 2 and 4.

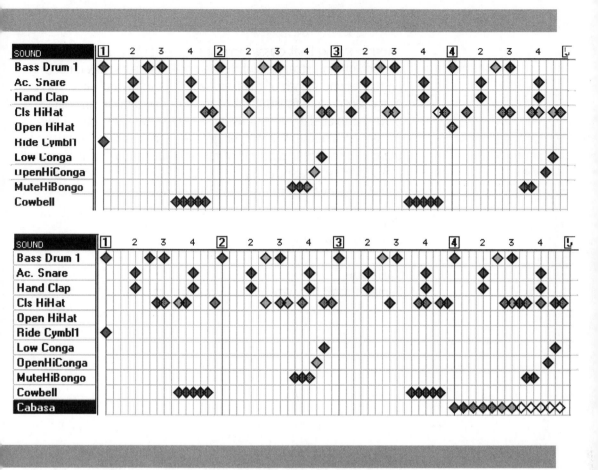

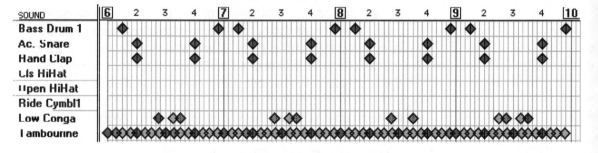

Dance/soul 8 (SMILEY)

Another swing-beat classic, this one uses a pretty unexciting hi hat pattern playing straight eighths on closed hat using open hat only on the second eighth of the first beat. The snare and claps play on every second and fourth beat of the bar. The tambourine pattern is playing triplet sixteenths (missing the second triplet) giving this pattern an irresistible swing or groove. The bass drum is busier than on most other patterns of this style in that, while it always plays the first beat of every bar, it also uses the last sixteenth triplet beat just before beats 2, 3 and 4 of the bar.

Fill
A very simple but effective fill.

Variation
Same as basic but with a crash cymbal at the start.

Dance/soul 9 (UNPLUGGD)

More swing-beat, this time with quite a bit more latin percussion courtesy of congas, go-go bells and tambourine playing a nicely syncopated sixteenth pattern. Snare plays beats 2 and 4 of the bar. Try doubling this with a nice clap sample. Bass drum always plays the first beat in the bar but uses a lot of up-beat sixteenths between beats making this pattern a real mover. The quantise or time correction used in this pattern is between straight and triplet sixteenths though closer to the straights. It's the very small hint of triplets that give this pattern its looseness.

Intro
Triplet sixteenth tambourine and hi hat pattern.

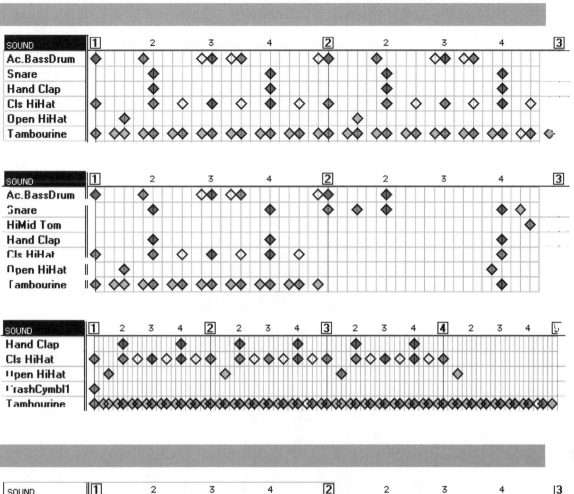

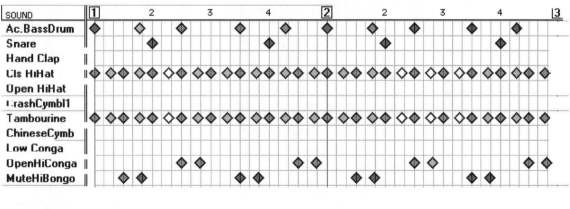

Dance/soul 10 (YOUHAVNT)

Straight sixteenth hi hats accented on every first and third sixteenth of the beat give this pattern its clubby 70s feel. The snare and claps play on every second and fourth beat of the bar while the bass drum plays a busy-ish up-beat sixteenth pattern, though it always plays the first beat of the bar.

SOUND	1	2	3	4	2	2	3	4	3
Ac.BassDrum									
Ac. Snare									
Hand Clap									
Cls HiHat									

4   *Jazz and world rhythms*

Used a lot in the 50s and 60s, this pattern is conspicuous for the absence of the snare drum. It features the mid-tom on every fourth pair of eighths of the bar, while the rim plays only beat 2 of every bar. The ride cymbal provides this pattern with its airiness playing a slightly broken sixteenth beat pattern and *always* missing the second sixteenth in the beat.

Fill
Low mounted tom in a ramped velocity eighth beat fill.

Triplet eighth jazz 1 (8TJAZZ01)

Rim shot or snare drum plays every second and fourth beat of the bar while the hi hat plays triplet eighth notes (missing the second and third triplet eighths). If the bass drum is used, it can play beats 1 and 3 of the bar. Notice the seemingly random accents later in the pattern which really show this pattern off to its full.

Fill
All in triplet eighth time – this fill really jumps.

Intro
A crash cymbal on every second beat of a bar adds excitement to this pattern while the ride plays airy triplet eighth beats.

Variation 1
Same as basic but snare breaks off into a flurry of triplet sixteenths and a crash and bass drum on the following bar at beat two.

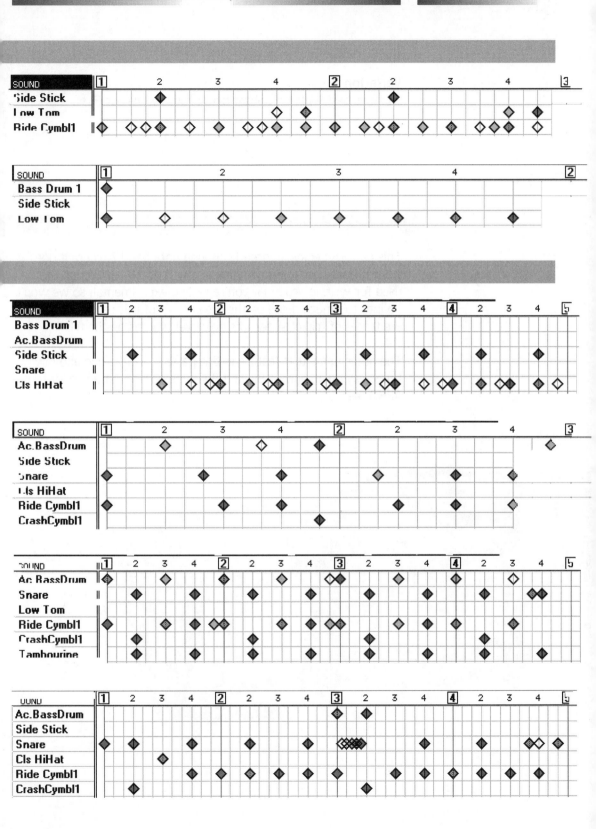

Triplet eighth jazz 1 (8TJAZZ01) – continued

Variation 2
Same as basic with an upbeat bass drum before bar 3.

Afro rock (AFROROCK)

This pattern begins innocently enough until bar 17 where it does what it does best – groove. Almost any 8 or 16 bar section can be used for writing around if you're feeling experimental, so we won't go into too much detail on the breakdown of this pattern. There are traces of triplet sixteenths or triplet eighths on the fills.

The other items that feature in this pattern are the mid and low toms playing an almost Bill and Ben type phrase but add a lot to its AFRO feel.

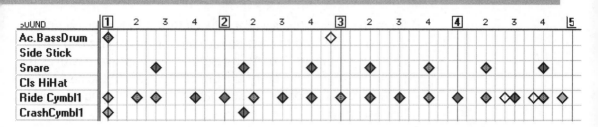

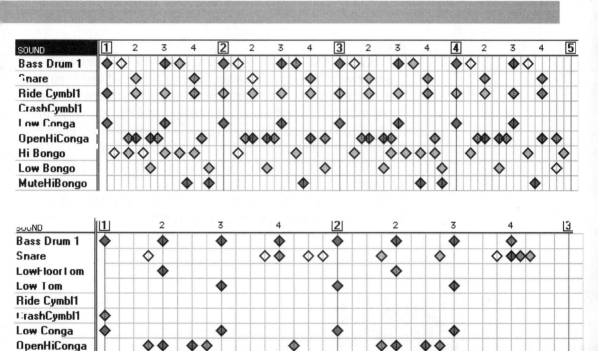

Be bop jazz 1 (BEBOP001)

From the likes of the legendary Buddy Rich, this is a typical (if such a word can be used to describe such a hot pattern) jazz bop riff. Again, try using any 8 or 16 bar section to jam or write with as the pattern changes from every eight or sixteen bars to the next. This pattern can fill a book with explanations of what's going on so just load and play!

Fill
A simple (?) fill pattern.

Intro
This features four bars of triplet sixteenth floor toms heavily accented with bass drum on every quarter note beat and hi hat on every upbeat eighth note finally concluding in the fourth bar with a flurry of 32nd ramped snare drum beats. Note that the snare fill starts at top velocity going down quickly then slowly fading up to full velocity by the end.

Variation
Most of the fancy stuff is on the snare where the left hand uses 'bounce fills' at various points in the pattern.

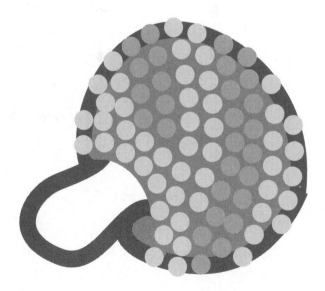

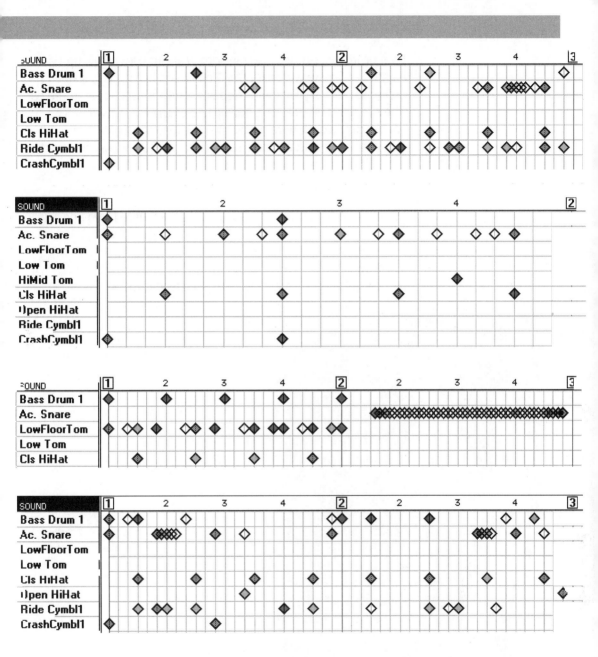

Bossanova 1 (BOSONOV1)

Bass drum plays every quarter note beat but uses a soft up-beat eighth before every down-beat. The closed hi hat plays sixteenths accented on every first and third sixteenth of every beat in the bar. The rim plays on beat only for beat 2 of the bar. Low and high congas play eighth note patterns. This style caught on fast, with many Latin-American songs in the 50s and 60s being composed around this style.

Fill
Eighth note fill pattern from snare to top mounted tom and finally to the floor tom.

Variation
Same as basic but using ride cymbal instead of hats.

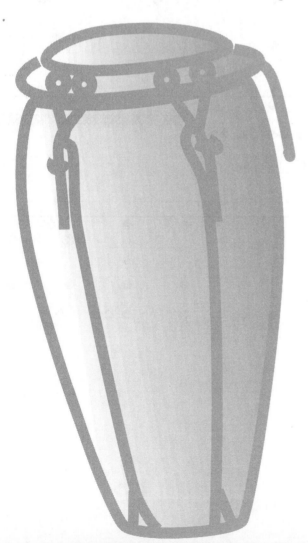

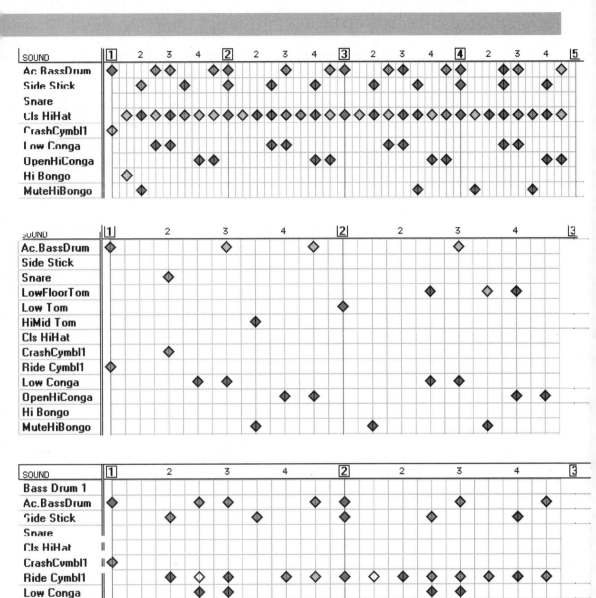

Calypso (CALYPSO)

This percussion riff is one of if not the favourite patterns of percussionist Ralph MacDonald. The bass drum starts out with a pretty average phrase moving into a straight quarter note groove as does the hi hat. Go-go bells play a continuous and hypnotic sixteenth beat phrase while the congas play a broken syncopated sixteenth beat phrase. All of this changes into a very funky drum and percussion pattern in the end. Try jamming or writing around any 8 or 16 bar section.

Fill

A very reserved snare fill. With what's happening elsewhere in this pattern, it pays not to get too busy with fills in this pattern as it is the percussion parts that are the features.

Variation

Straight four bass drums and closed hats with snare at beats 2 and 4.

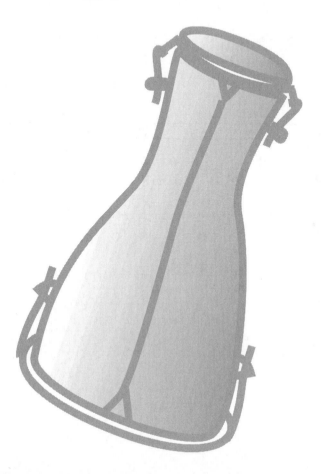

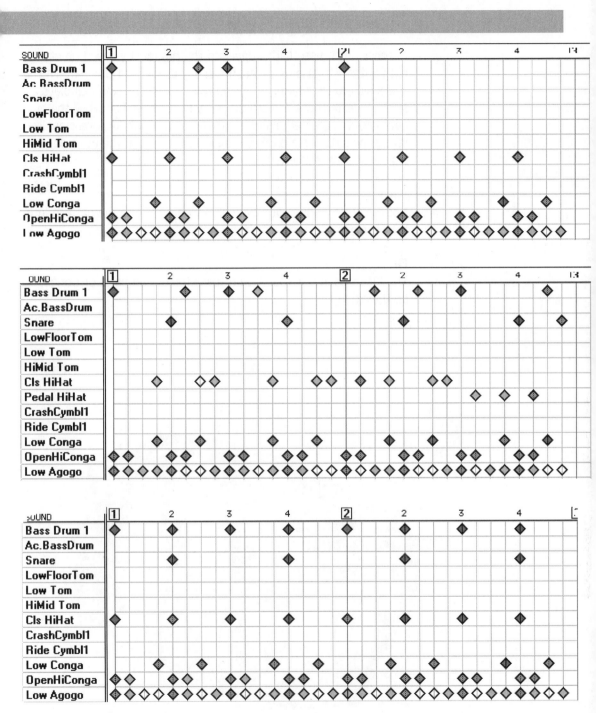

Cha cha 1a (CHACHA1A)

Another much used Latin-American rhythm mostly based on eighth note beats. The use of sixteenths in any element of this pattern can add a nice touch so long as it's not overdone. The cow bell plays a steady quarter note pattern on every beat of the bar while the hi hat plays an accented eighth note phrase throughout, occasionally lifting the left foot a bit for a semi open hi hat on the up-beat eighth of beat 3 of the bar.

Fill 1
Not really a fill – just ride cymbal in eighths taking the pattern into the next bar.

Fill 2
The kit stops at bar four giving space for the timbales or bongos to do their thing.

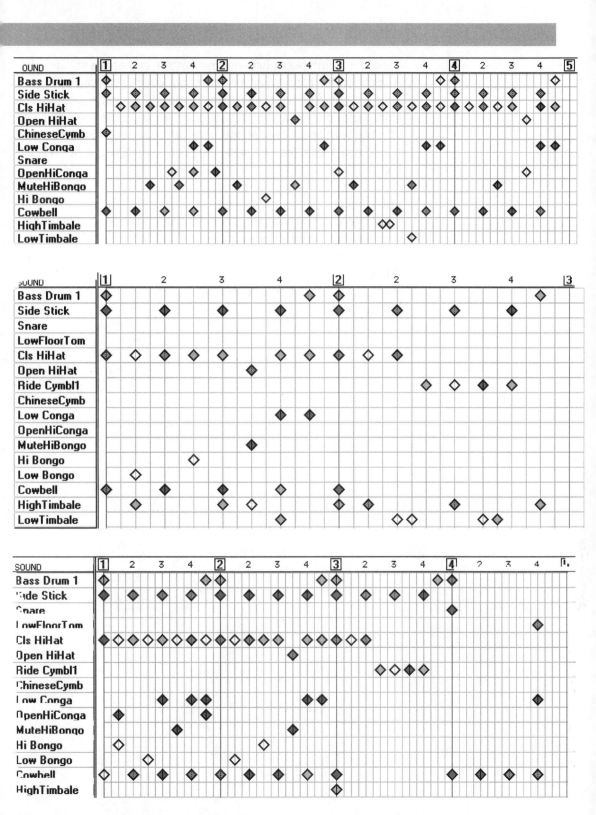

Latin ballad 1 (L_BALLD1)

Based on eighth note phrasing, this pattern provides a steady solid foundation for Latin type ballads and has even been used by the likes of Santana from time to time. Closed hi hat plays a straight eighth beat phrase while the bass drum always plays the first beat of a bar with an up-beat eighth note before beats 3 and 1 of the bar. The rim shot (or side-stick) plays on beats 2 and 4 of every bar.

Fill 1
Viewed in pairs of two bars – this fill simply stops at bar two with a single strike on the floor tom at beat four of bar two.

Fill 2
Works as a build up to a double time pattern as the snare breaks into sixteenths.

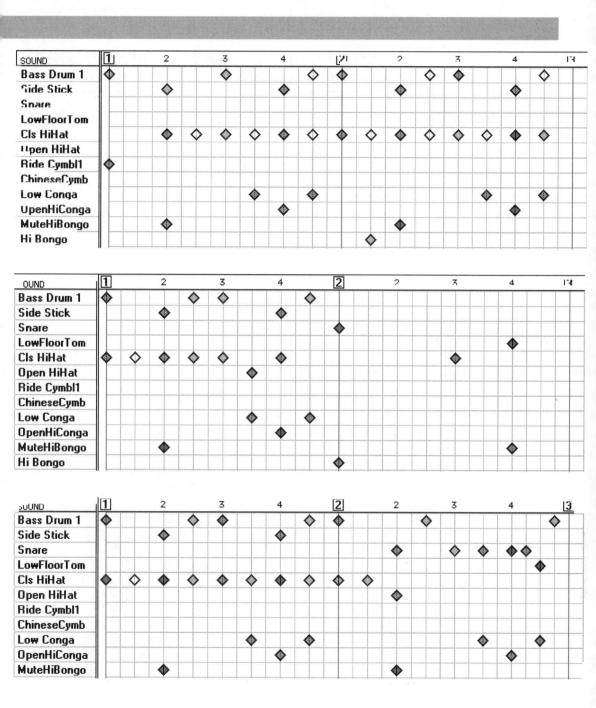

Latin ballad 2 (L_BALLD2)

A variation on the last pattern, this one begins with a fill using the whole kit and mixing eights and sixteens before settling down to the main pattern which uses bongo rolls to give an almost mysterious feel to the phrase.

Fill
A simple tom fill combining eighths and sixteenths.

Variation
Same as basic without the flurried bongos.

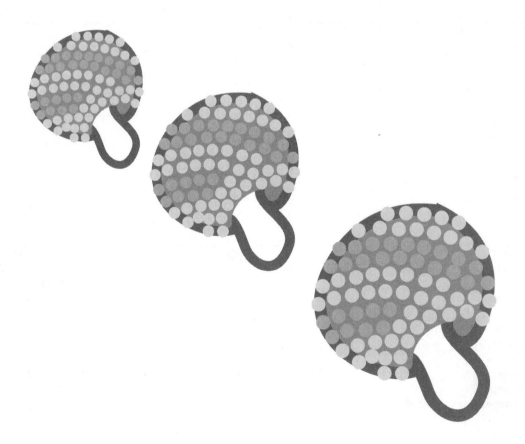

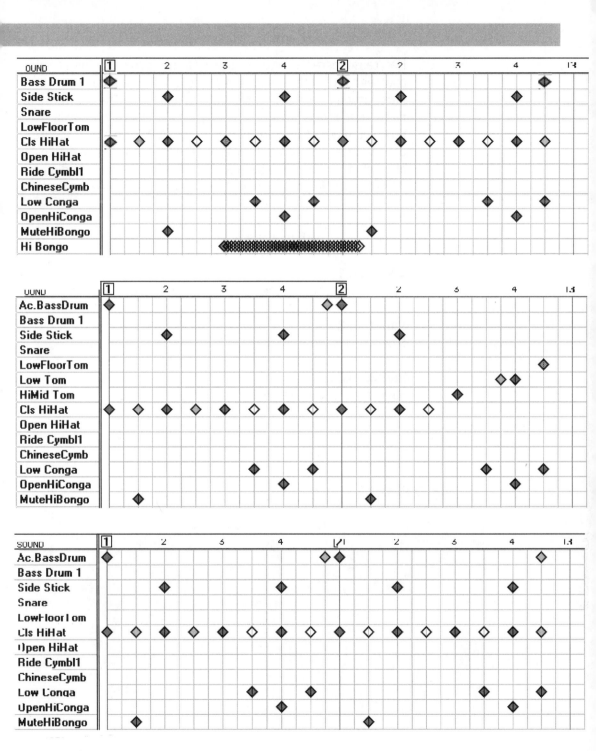

Mambo 1 (MAMBO_01)

Not 'cause there's a hispanic involved in this book, but this is yet another heavily used percussion phrase still in use today since its introduction to popular music over 40 years ago! The quarter note bass drum phrase helps to westernise it a bit more while still retaining much of its original feel, thanks to the dominant nature of the congas and cow bell phrases. The broken hi hat sixteenths also help to tribe it up a bit. For a more detailed understanding of what's happening in the congas department, see the pattern grid.

Fill
Same as basic with timbales playing eighth beat fills.

Variation 1
The floor tom adds some rumble to the low end.

Variation 2
More rumble from the low and floor toms.

Variation 3
Same as basic but uses ride cymbal instead of hats.

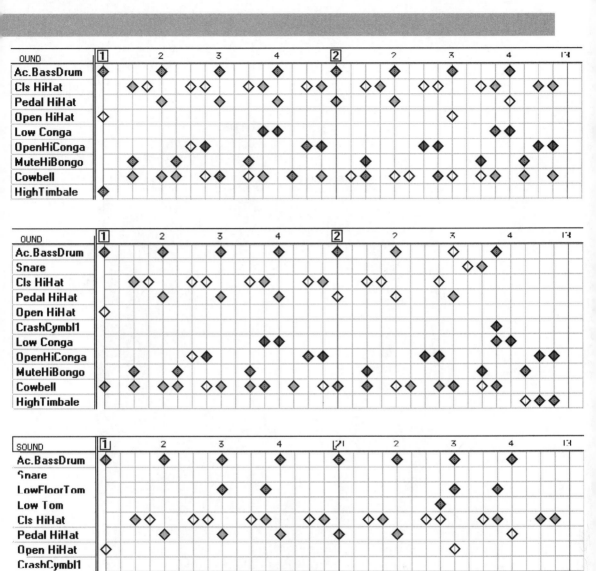

Mambo 1 (MAMBO_01) – continued

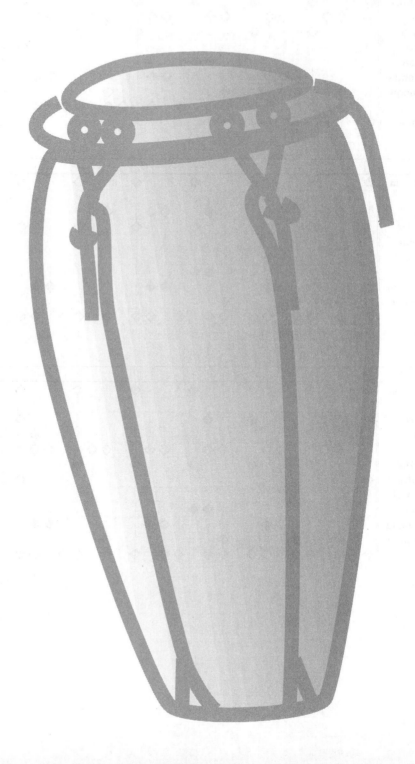

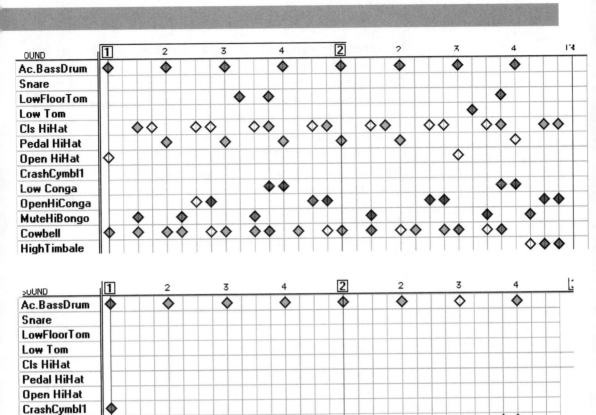

Merengue (MERENGUE)

If you're a latin band and your repertoire does not include a piece of music using this rhythm – quit now! The Merengue is a Dominican rhythm with a long history for waking spirits in the most introverted of musicians – and dancers. One reason for this could be to do with its density of accented sixteenth beat phrases and the droning rasp of the guiro – a hand held wooden percussion instrument played with what looks like an Afro comb. The congas in this instance may as well be played using heavy sticks as opposed to the usual hands.

Variation 1
Timbales playing choppy sixteenths add some spice to this variation.

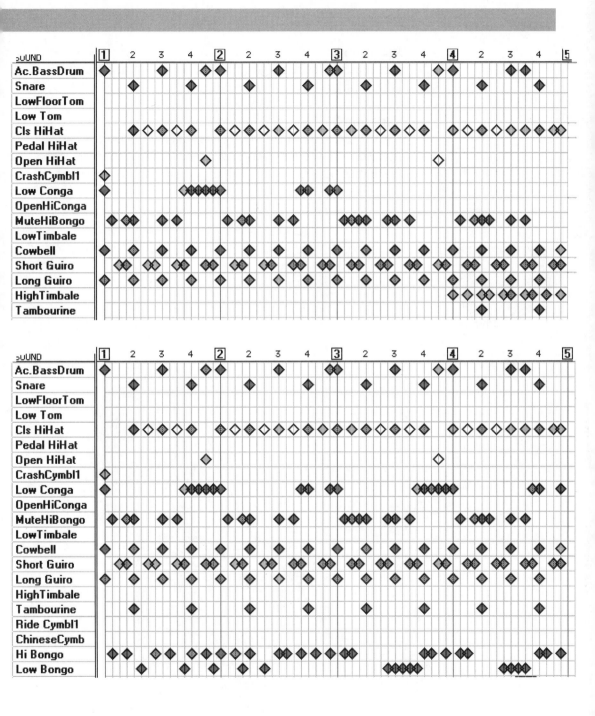

Merengue (MERENGUE) – continued

Variation 2

Some tasty combination eighth and sixteenth beat bongo improvisation.

Variation 3

Can't forget the congas which can break away from the basic pattern to do some riff work without sacrificing the bulk of the feel in this pattern.

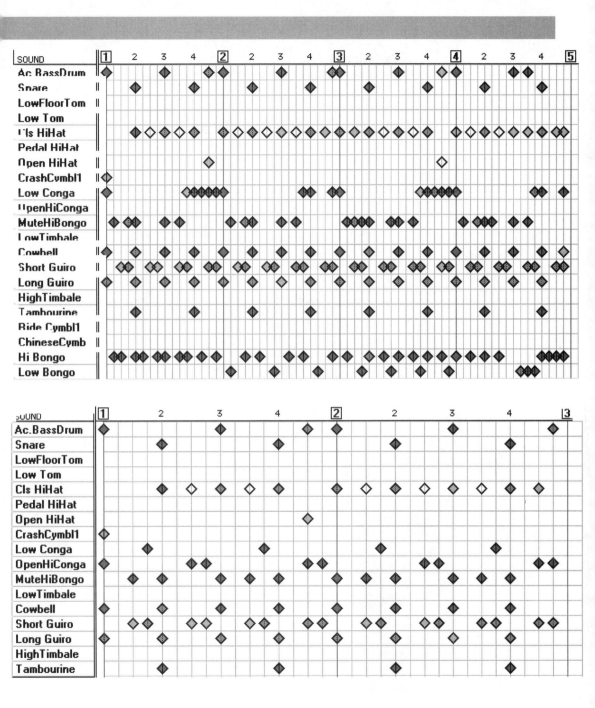

Merengue (MERENGUE) – continued

Variation 4
Same as basic but uses a crash cymbal at the start.

Fill
A typical merengue fill in broken sixteenths.

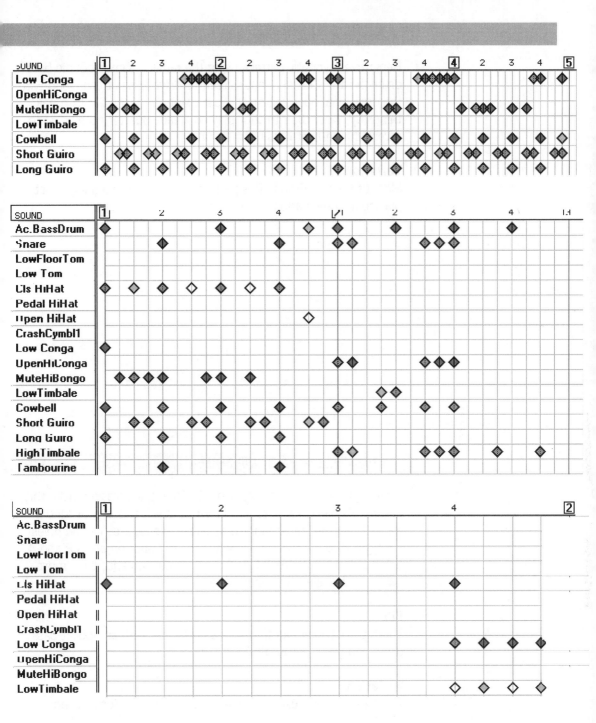

Mozambique (MOZAMBIK)

Repetitive, hypnotic pattern using the familiar samba double bass drum phrase. Closed hi hat sixteenths drive this pattern along with the occasional open hat on the last sixteenth of the bar to break things up. Note the rim shot playing steady quarter note beats to accent the on-beat bass drum phrase.

Variation
Most of the variation in this pattern comes from the bongo part playing in combinations of upbeat eighth and sixteenths.

Quick triplet sixteens 2 (QUIK16T2)

Heavy syncopations, accents and HOLES in the phrasing make this pattern absolute magic to jam or write to – if this is your kind of thing. Based on triplet eighths at a fast tempo, accents and holes cut right through this phrase while the rim shot on beats 2 and 4 help to stabilise the feel. Latin swing percussion adds even more swing to this already swingy style.

Fill
Snare plays triplet eighth upbeats in last bar with an upbeat bass drum and crash before the next bar.

Variation
Same as basic but uses snare instead of side stick (or rim shot).

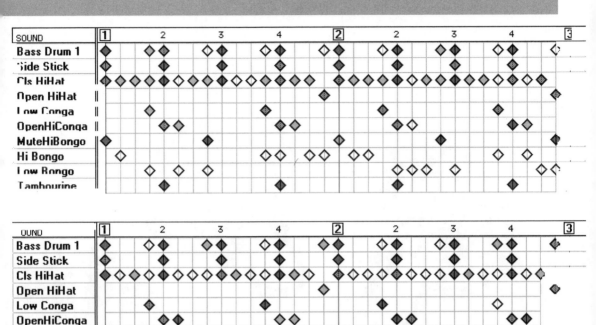

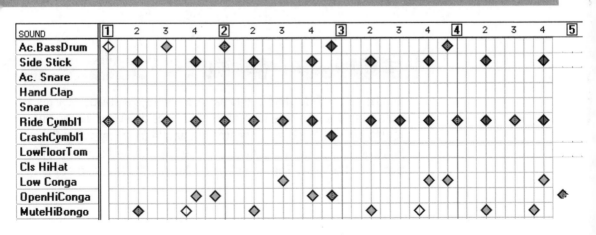

Quick triplet sixteens 2 (QUIK16T2) – continued

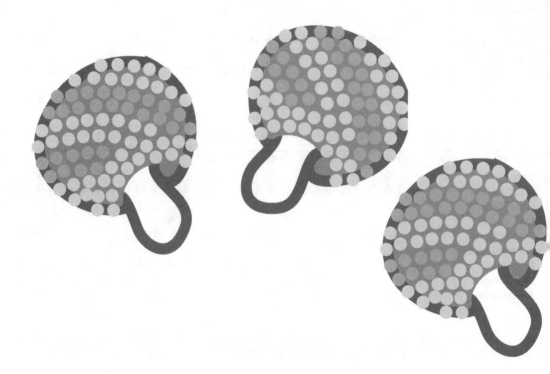

Quick triplet sixteens 4 (QUIK16T4)

Similar to the QUIK16T2, this pattern employs a steady quarter note bass drum phrase with snare and claps on every second and fourth beat of the bar. Sixteenths are ample for most fancy fill work which can begin anywhere in the bar and perhaps even spill over into the next. The ride plays triplet eighths (missing out a few).

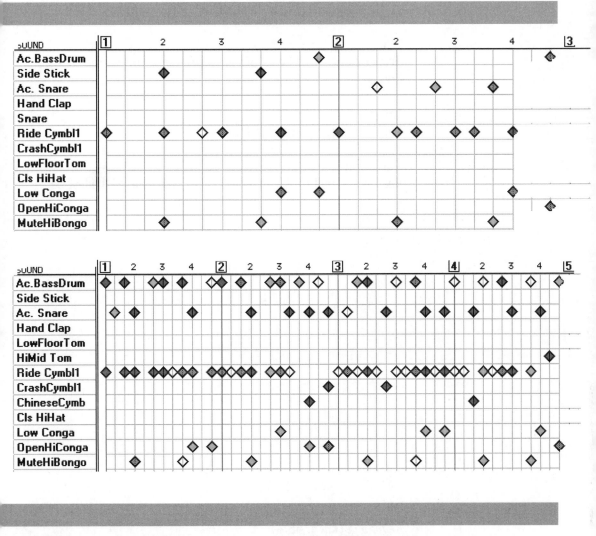

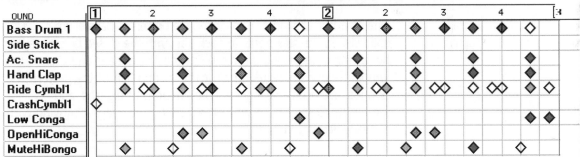

Quick triplet sixteens 4 (QUIK16T4) – continued

Fill
Triplet eighth note beats off the snare make this pattern really boogie.

Intro
Velocity ramped sixteenth snare drum fill.

Variation
Features a mini triplet sixteenth fill at beat four of the last bar.

Reggae 1a (REGGAE1A)

One of if not *the* most used of reggae patterns. Bass drum plays solid steady quarter notes in each bar with the closed hi hat playing heavily accented eighths for the first half of the bar and then jumping around in sixteenths for the second half of the pattern. Bongos are used sparingly in combinations of eighths and sixteenths to spice it up while the tambourine keeps it moving with a steady accented eighth note phrase.

Intro
Same as basic pattern using only closed/open hi hat and bass drum.

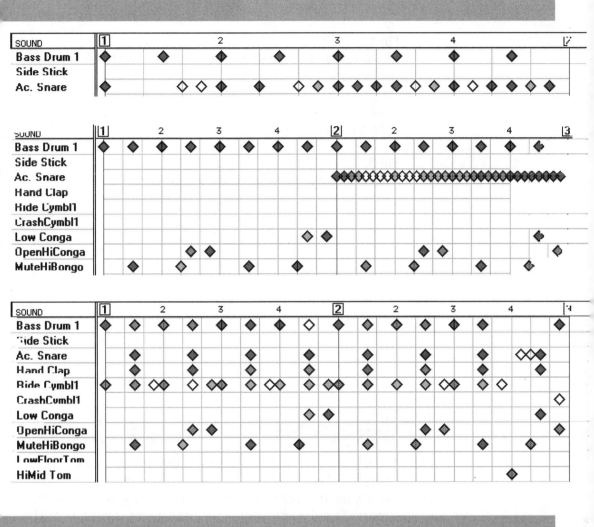

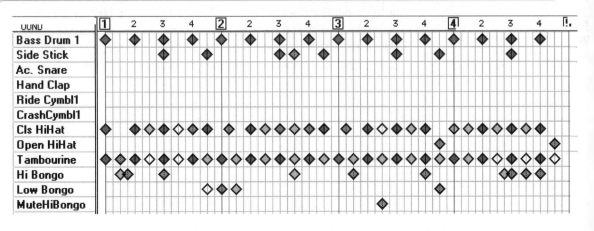

Reggae 1a (REGGAE1A) – continued

Fill 1

All but the tambourine drops out for this one while the bongos do the fill work.

Fill 2

Upbeat sixteenths from hi mounted tom to floor tom.

Fill 3

Simple upbeat eighth snare and crash cymbal.

Reggae 2a (REGGAE2A)

This one is based on triplet sixteenths throughout – especially where the hi hat is concerned. The bass drum plays the first beat for only the first bar in a 16 bar phrase – maybe not ever again after the first until the very end. What happens instead, is, the bass drum plays on beats 2 and 4 of the bar with the occasional eighth note up-beats of beats 1 and 3. The rim joins the bass drum on beats 2 and 4 of the bar but is free to indulge itself in syncopated sixteenths almost anywhere in the bar. Tambourine is just incidental to the rest of the instruments but you'd miss it if it wasn't there.

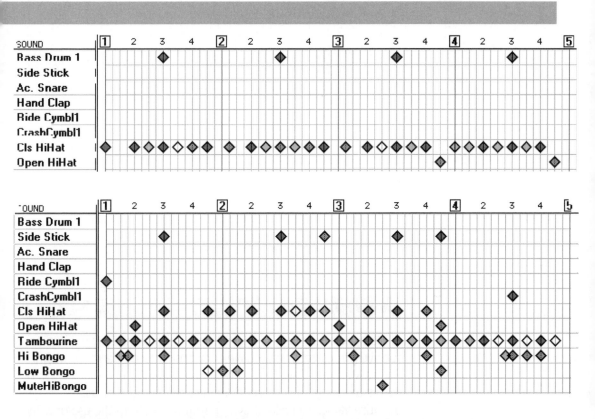

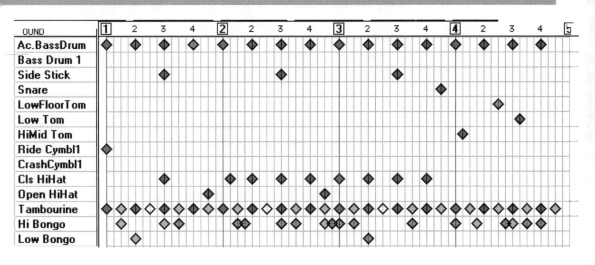

Reggae 2a (REGGAE2A) – continued

Rhumba 1 (RHUMBA01)

Made popular in the 50s and 60s, the rhumba has formed the basis for everything from the I Love Lucy theme to modern day Miami Sound Machine. This pattern resembles Mambo in a lot of ways but seems to swing a bit more. Try small percentages of triplet quantise values to make it swing even more. Note the use of 32nd notes in the fills. Of special interest – take at look at the not too busy timbale solo and check out the syncopations used.

Intro
Chopped up sixteenth break beat intro using hi timbale, hi open conga and cow bell.

Fill 1
The last bar features a combination of triplet and straight sixteenth beats on the hi open conga and hi timbale.

Fill 2
Another favourite latin break with the hi timbale rolling out into the next bar.

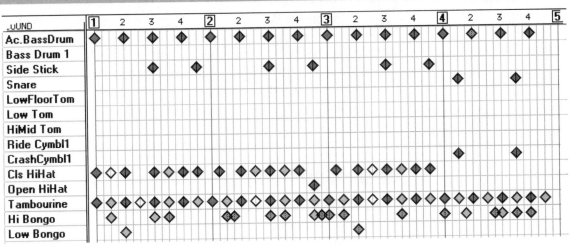

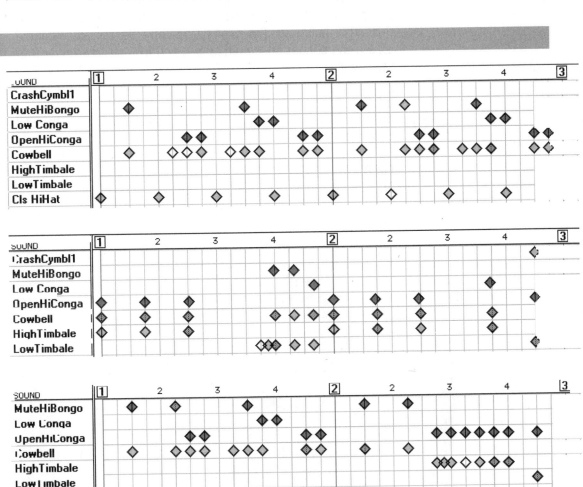

Rhumba 2 (RHUMBA02)

A variation on RHUMBA01. This pattern can be used for a 'verse' part. Also good at backing a jazzy piano solo. Note the spurious use of bongos and the effect imposed by the tiny clave. This all builds up to the middle to end section where large and small cowbells are used to really push the beat home. A bass drum and crash cymbal may be used on the first bar of a 16 or 32 bar section. Note also, the 32nds used in the timbale fills.

Samba 2a (SAMBA_2A)

As Brazilian as Tanya Maria, this pattern oozes South America. The bass drum plays every quarter note but syncopates a sixteenth before every one of those quarters. The sparse ride cymbal and sixteenth note shaker phrases almost give music the quality of floating or bouncing. The small percussion – i.e. the go-go bells, cabasa and bongos lift it even higher. An infectious rhythm at the very least.

Fill 1
The drum kit keeps it simple with bass drum and ride cymbal while congas and bongos do the rest.

Fill 2
Another simple fill using the mid tom.

Fill 3
A more spicy fill using snare and floor tom in sixteenths.

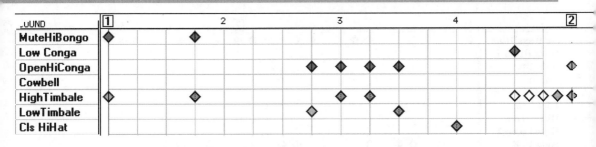

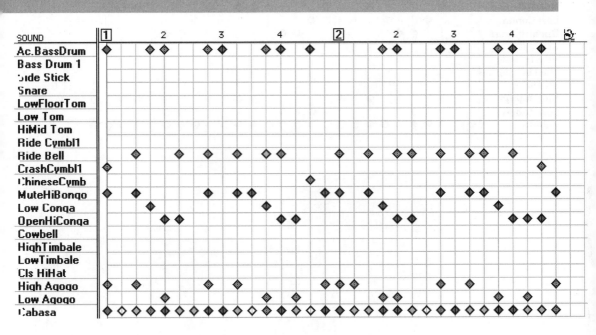

Samba 2a (SAMBA_2A) – continued

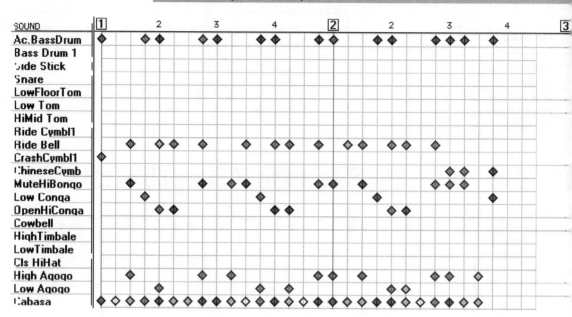

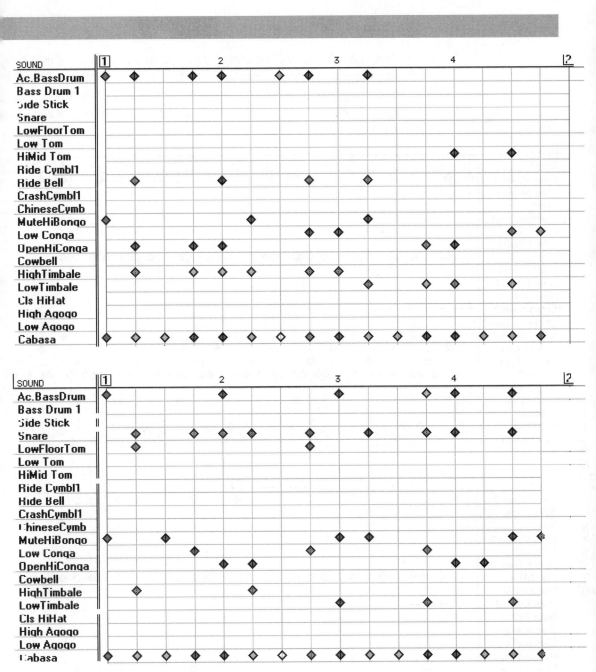

Santana 1 (SANTANA1)

What else can you call something that sounds and feels like this?
Note the almost tribal phrasing of the bass drum accented by the
sixteenth hi hat and cowbell phrase. Note the unusual (to the
layman) syncopated up-beat sixteenths played by the bongos and
timbales.

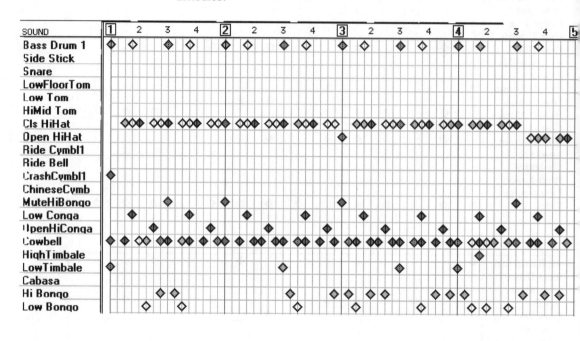

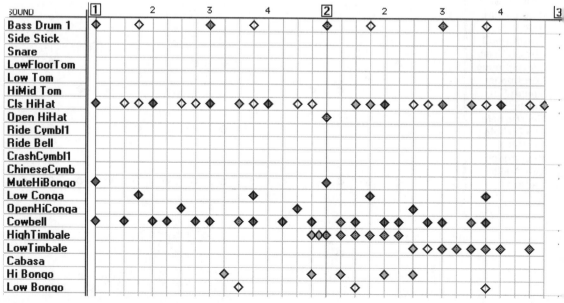

Fill

The drum kit stays steady on the beat while the timbale track does the fancy stuff.

Variations

In Variation 1, the drum kit is still steady – the variation is in the percussion tracks but it sounds like another pattern altogether. In Variation 2 at long last the drum track takes on another form as the snare begins to introduce some upbeat sixteenths beats.

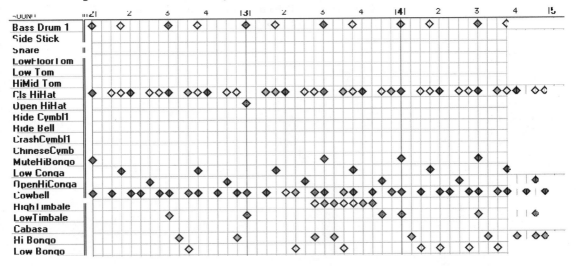

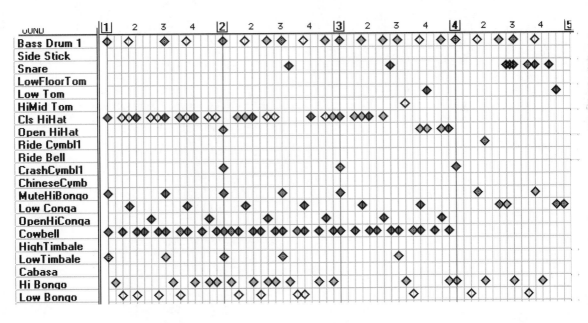

Soca 1 (SOCA_1)

From Trinidad to Barbados to Carnival in London – here is another Caribbean delicacy – soca. Similar in small ways to West Africa's High Life rhythms. Good for middle percussion breaks or even endings. The bass drum plays straight quarter notes while the snare brushes in syncopated sixteenths. The hi hat is only being pedalled by the drummer's left foot on the up-beat of every quarter note in the bar.

Variation
Same as basic but uses a snare and crash cymbal on the fourth upbeat sixteenth of the bar.

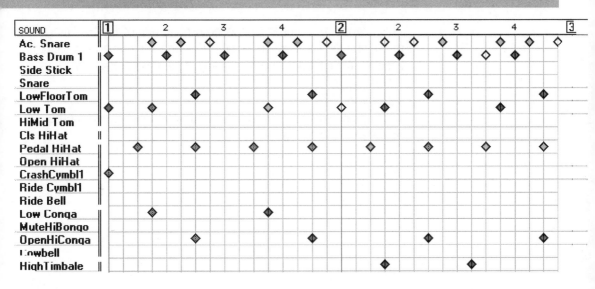

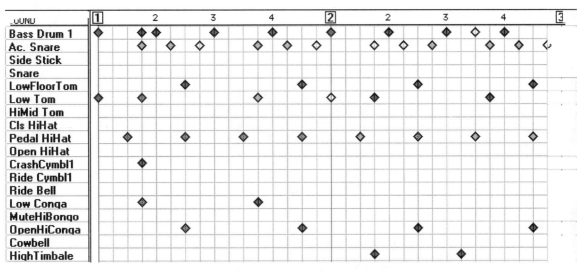

Soca 2 (SOCA_2)

This flavour of soca has even been used in one of Herbie Hancock's dance hits. Not as busy as Soca 1, this one still manages a saucy groove. Try jamming or writing around any 8 bar section.

Variation
Uses upbeat sixteenth snare, mid and floor toms joined by the timbales in the fourth bar.

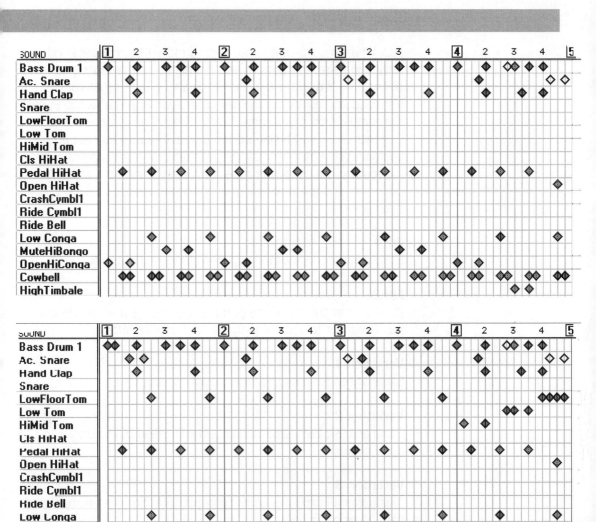

Just when you thought it was safe to move out of triplets and into something else, this pattern was a must to include amongst this collection – if only for the artistry displayed in the footwork and left hand playing snare. The swingy conga pattern is just icing but the combination is awesome. You'll always find an accented snare on beats 2 and 4. The bass drum only sees a quarter beat at the beginning of a bar – for the rest of the bar – it syncopates in triplet sixteenths. The hi hat work has a lot in common with what's going on in the bass drum phrase missing the second triplet 16 per quarter note.

Fill 1
Simple fill on snare and hi mid tom at the end of the bar.

Fill 2
It looks over the top in the grid but it sounds just wicked in the file. Great for taking the song into a chorus or middle 8.

Variation 1
Same as basic but begins with a crash cymbal.

Variation 2
Same as basic but uses the ride cymbal instead of the closed and open hi hats.

Variation 3
This pattern introduces some syncopation in both the snare and bass drum parts.

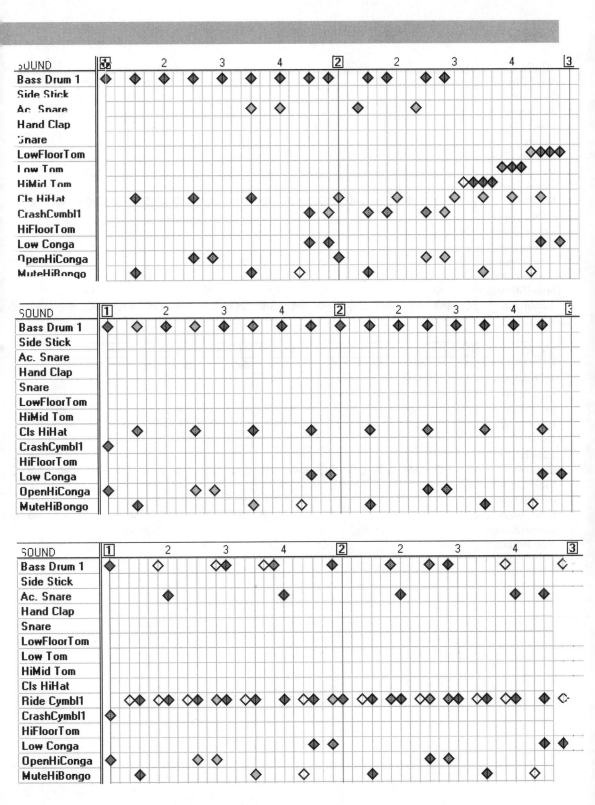

Triplet sixteenth swing (16TSWING) – continued

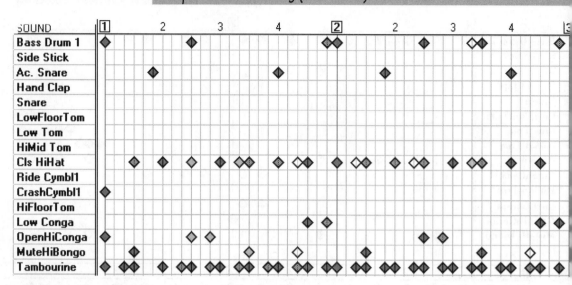

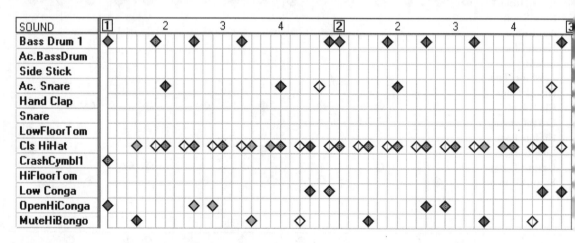

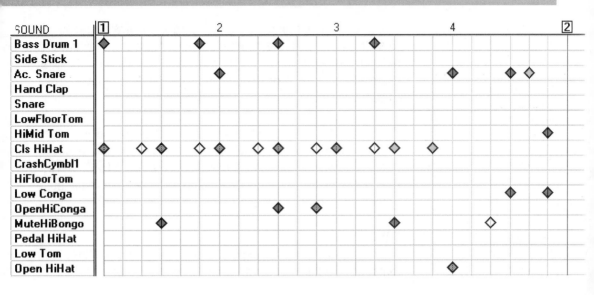

Eights 1 (EIGHTSO1)

A mid tempo drum and percussion phrase for anything from rock to MOR. Also good as a general purpose backbeat. This pattern builds from one using a rim shot on beat 2 of the bar. The bass drum accents beat 1 of the bar and syncopates in eighths. The closed hi hat plays beats 1, 3 and 4.

For the main groove, we bring the snare and tambourine in on beats 2 and 4 of the bar and the hi hat is now playing quarter notes while the congas play a chacha phrase (see CHACHA1A). The bass drum always accents beats 1 and 3 of the bar with light syncopated eighths between beats 3 and 4 of the bar.

Fill
Simple eighth beat fill using snare and lo tom. The rattling tambourine adds a sense of suspense to this pattern.

Intro (below)
Crash – bang – wallop as the congas flurry in a 32 beat fill, the toms take it nice and easy with a straight eighth fill.

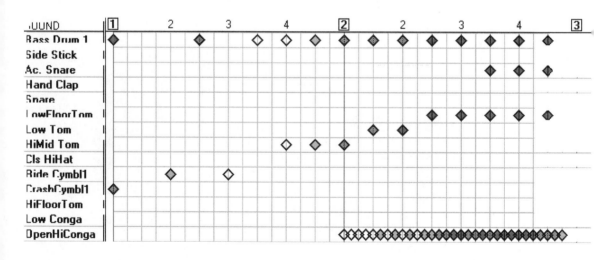

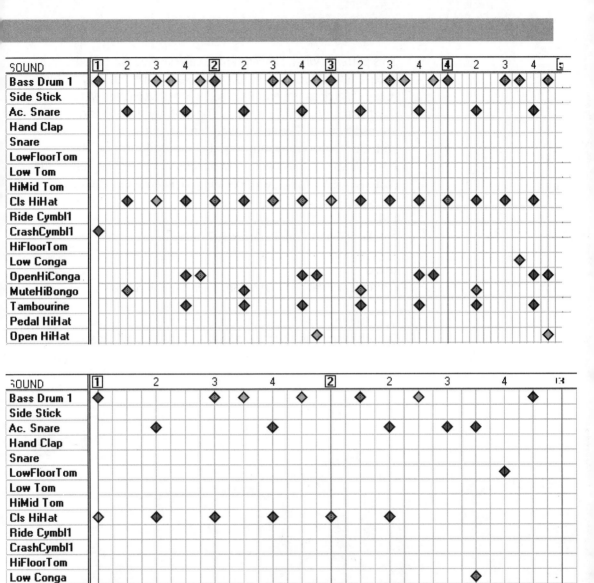

Funk rock 1 (FUNKROK1)

This pattern, when slowed down, can be used for ballads. At its programmed tempo, it feels more like the filename says – funky – rocky. The closed hi hat plays sixteenths, accenting every first and third sixteenth, which accounts for the way the top end almost seems to pump. The snare plays the mandatory beat 2s and 4s with the occasional eighth or sixteenth used for fills. The introduction of the congas and bongos in the second half of the pattern shows how the whole thing really comes together.

Fill
Simple sixteenth fill on snare and hi tom.

Intro
A simple sixteenth fill in on snare and hi mid tom.

Variation
Sparse congas and bongos round this pattern off nicely.

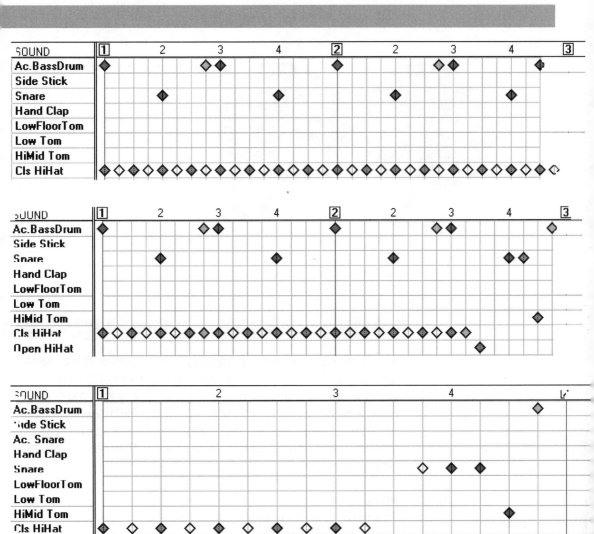

Funk rock 1 (FUNKROK1) – continued

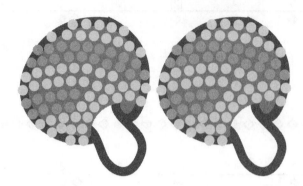

Hard eights 1 (HARD_8_1)

A solid steady rock beat for anything from Adams to Floyd. For the first half of the file, the bass drum plays quarter notes to the bar with the standard snare on beats 2 and 4. The hi hats move this along with eighth notes. In the middle of the file, the hi hat starts to rattle half open – which really adds impact to a section. The crash is used a lot more in this style of music than has previously been discussed.

Intro
This intro fill starts with an upbeat pickup on the bass drum followed by a sixteenth snare/bass drum fill on the next bar.

Fill 1
A simple build up on bass drum, snare and tom.

Variation 1
Same as basic but uses the ride cymbal instead if hat.

Variation 2
Snares on every quarter beat a la Motown help feed some drive into this variation.

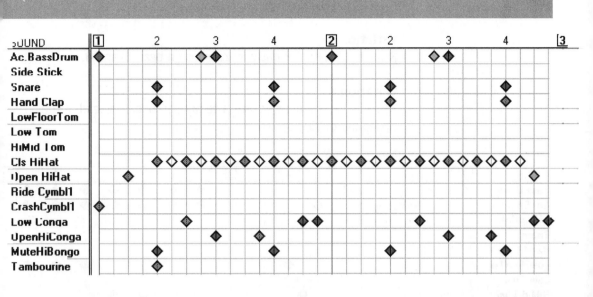

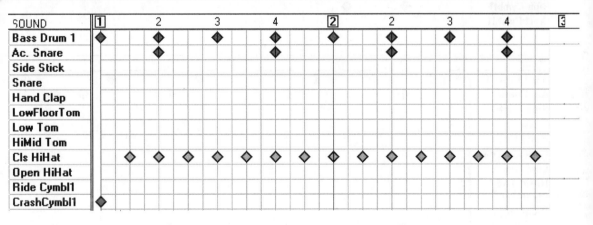

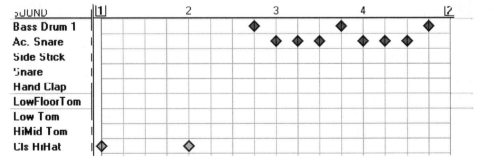

Hard eights 1 (HARD_8_1) – continued

Variation 3
Same as Variation 2 but with crashes on beats 3 and 4.

Variation 4
Same as Variation 1 but uses a semi open hi hat instead of the closed hat or ride cymbal.

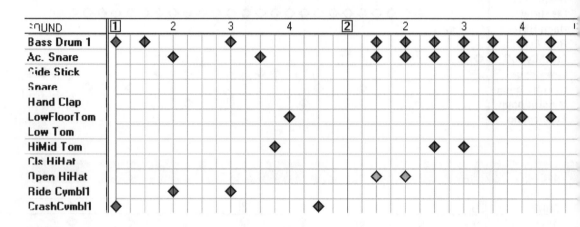

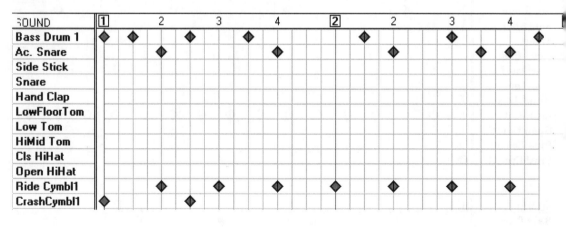

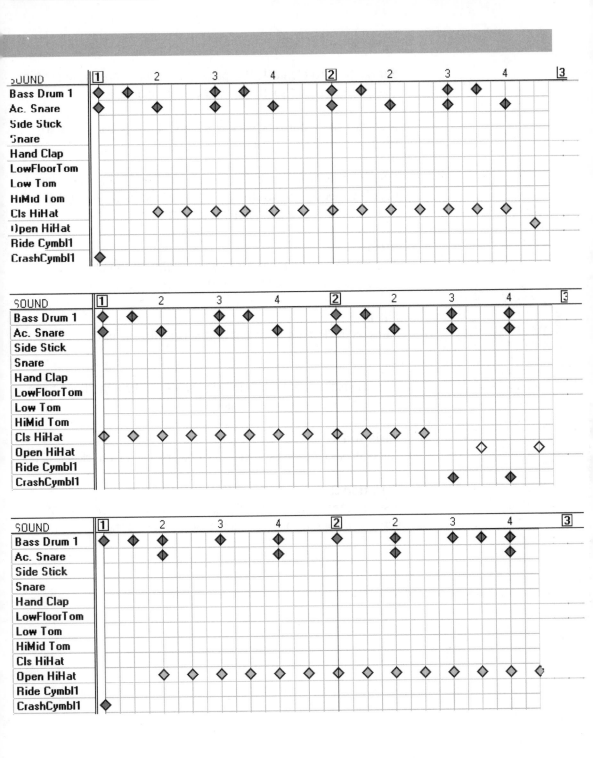

Hard eights 2 (HARD_8_2)

Similar to hard eights 1, this pattern has a bit more movement in the bass drum and so is rockier than hard eights 1.

Standard snare phrasing on beats 2 and 4 of the bar. Claps are used on beat 2 of the bar.

Check out the wild cymbal work and snare and tom fills in the middle to second half of the file. It's the kind of variation that can make a section of a song jump right out of your system.

Intro
This fill features in many Motown hits with its combination of straight eighths, sixteenths and triplet sixteenths.

Fill 1
Same as INTRO but leads out of one bar into the next.

Fill 2
A simple eighth beat build up using snare, hi, low and floor toms. A good fill into a chorus or middle 8.

Variation 1
Same as basic but uses the ride cymbal instead of the closed hi hat.

Variation 2
A syncopated bass drum and crash cymbal adds an element of surprise during a solo or middle 8 section of a song.

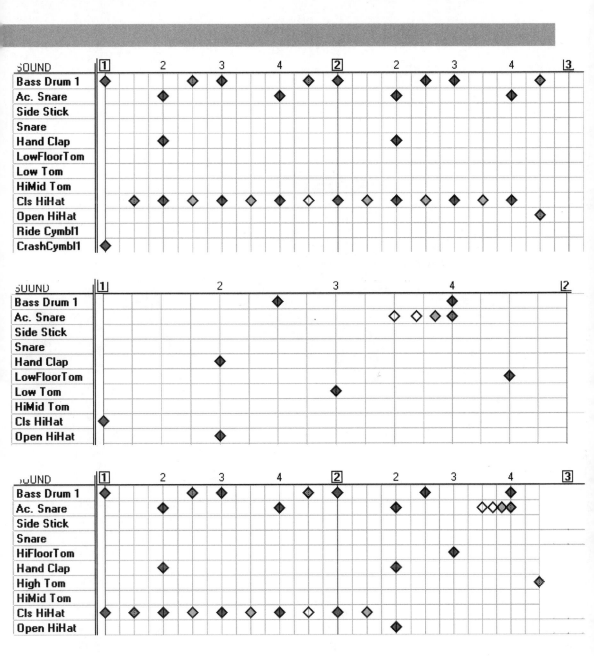

Hard eights 2 (HARD_8_2) – continued

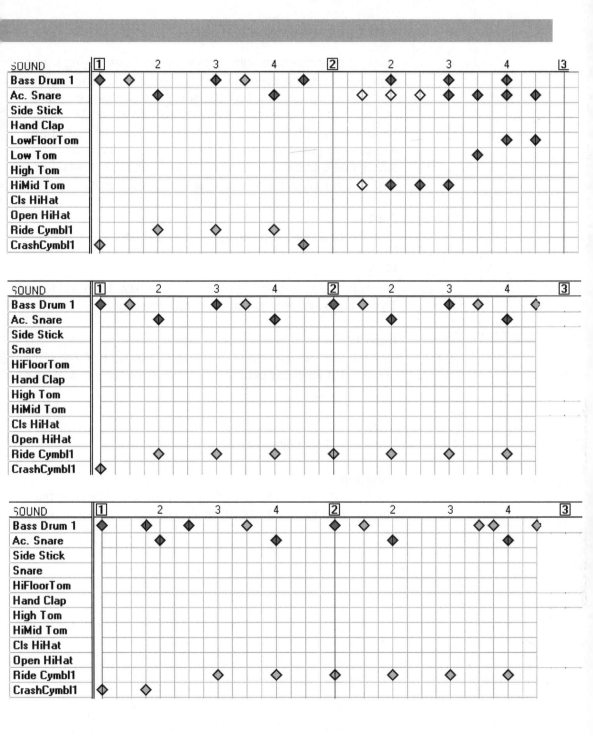

Hard triplet eighths (HARD_8T_)

The bass drum plays straight fours with the hi hat playing triplet eighths accented on the first of every three triplets. The toms are lightly accented using up-beat triplet eighths building up to ... the *buildup*. The ride takes over the hi hat pattern at bar 21 (excluding the count-in) with four quarter notes to the bar. The bass drum also changes phrasing with accents on beats 1 and 3 with syncopated triplet eighths between beats 1 and 3 and beat 1 of the next bar. The crash is also used liberally for excitement.

Fill 1
Straight triplet eighth fill on hi mid, low and floor toms.

Fill 2
All round the houses on this combination of bass drum and toms. This is a good fill in or out of a section of a song.

Intro 1
Straight fours on the bass drum along with triplet eighths on the closed hi hat keep this pattern steady while the toms play around on the upbeats.

Intro 2
More upbeat tom hits.

Variation
The crash cymbal on beats 1 of the first bar and upbeats in the next bar help to push this pattern along.

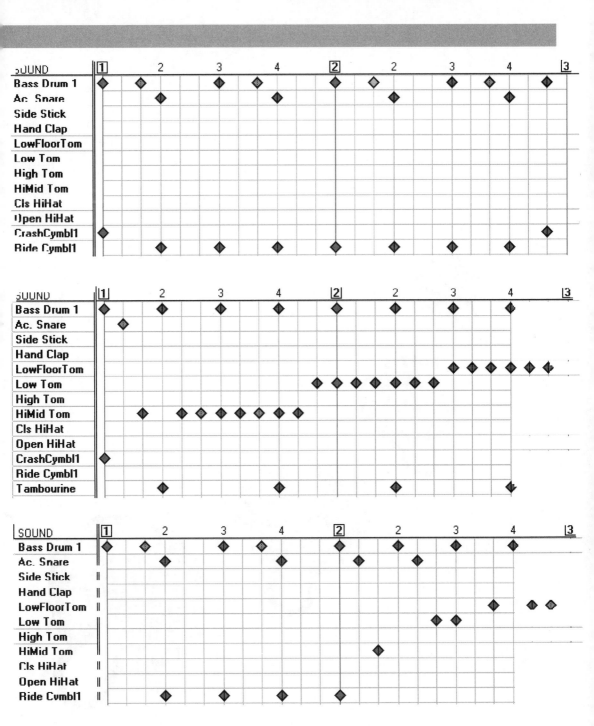

Hard triplet eighths (HARD_8T_) – continued

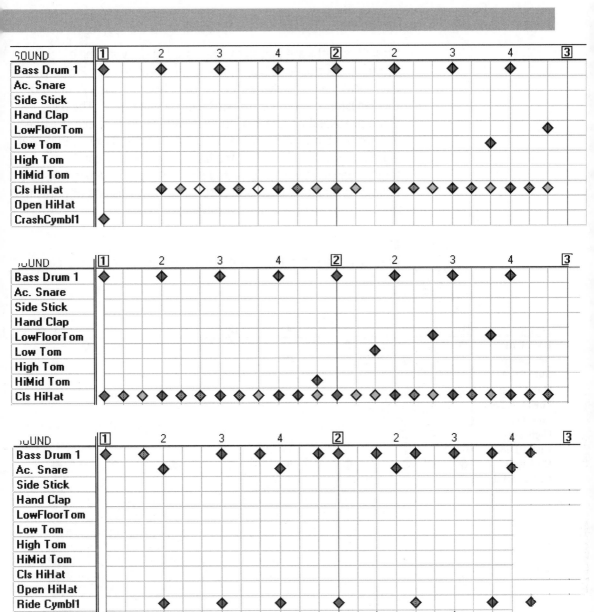

Quick fours b (QUIK_4_B)

Straight eighths are played by the closed hi hat with the exception of the up-beat open hi hat on beat eight (beat 4 – bar 2 of a two bar block); snare as always for the back beat on beats 2 and 4 of the bar later joined on the same beats by hand claps. The bass drum plays beats 1 and 3 of the bar with an up-beat eighth at beat 7 (beat 3 – bar 2 of a two bar block) and perhaps even an up-beat eighth on the fourth beat of the last bar into a new bar. The tambourine lightly plays accented eighth notes to the bar. This is another example of how latin percussion (towards end of pattern) puts even more groove into something.

Basic 2

Breaks at the second bar with simple straight fours on the bass drum.

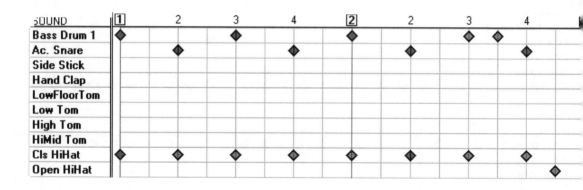

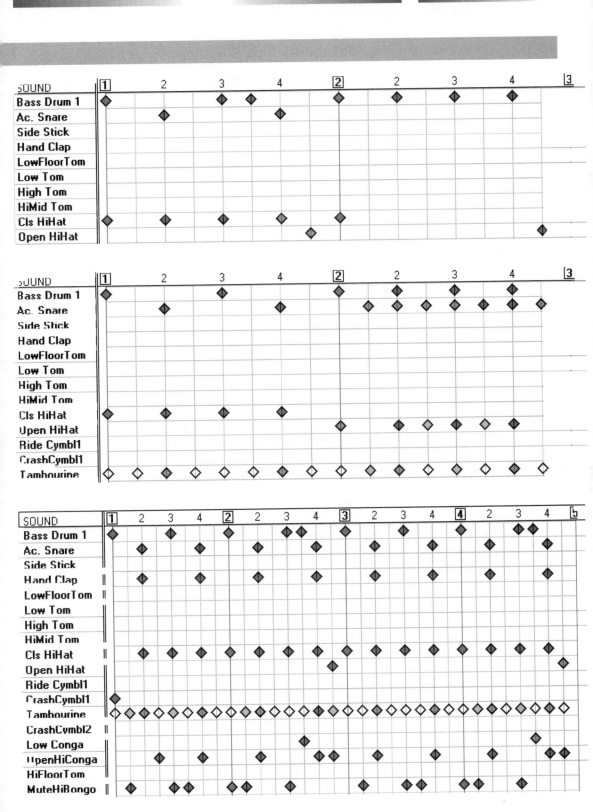

Quick triplet eights 1 (QUIK_8T1)

More like a souly raunchy rocky beat. The bass drum plays every quarter note in a bar with the closed hi hat playing triplet eighths accenting every first triplet eighth. Snare drum plays beats 2 and 4 as do the claps. Triplet tom fills make a good variation used sparingly.

Fill 1
A triplet eighth tom fill.

Fill 2
Same as Fill 1 but begins earlier on beat 1 of bar 2.

Variation
Same as the basic but with an extra triplet eighth on the bass drum at the upbeat of the third beat every other bar.

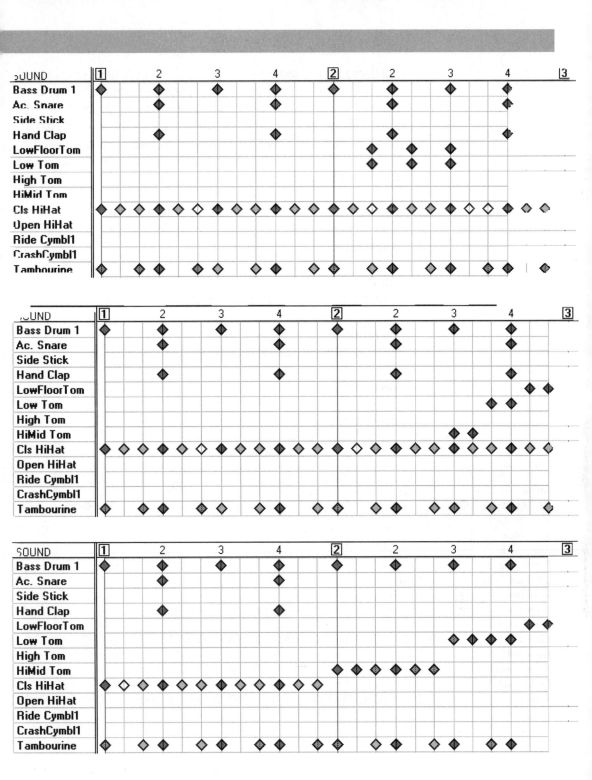

Rock ballad 1 (ROCKBAL1)

Solid steady sixteenth note focus of this drum pattern using a loosish tambourine phrase. Snare drum plays on beats 2 and 4 as does the rim shot when it is used. The closed hi hat plays steady eighths only occasionally opening up on the up-beat of the seventh beat (beat 3 – bar 2 of a two bar phrase). Accented eighths make up the general feel of the fills. Note the use of the open hi hat towards the end of the pattern.

Fill 1

A semi dramatic fill using snare, bass drum and toms with some added splash of crash cymbals.

Fill 2

A simple fill using low and floor toms.

Variation 1

Same as basic but uses a syncopated bass drum.

Variation 2

Same as Variation 1 but introduces the tambourine playing in sixteenths.

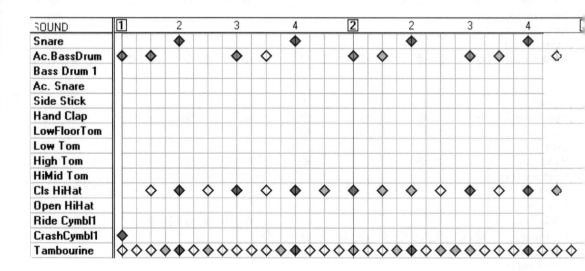

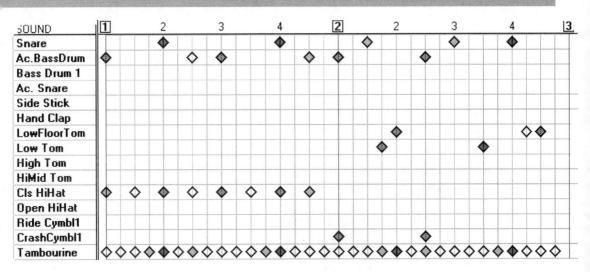

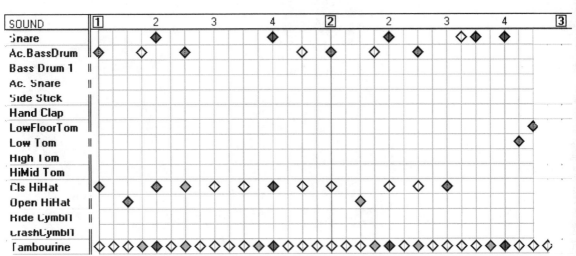

Rock ballad 1 (ROCKBAL1) – continued

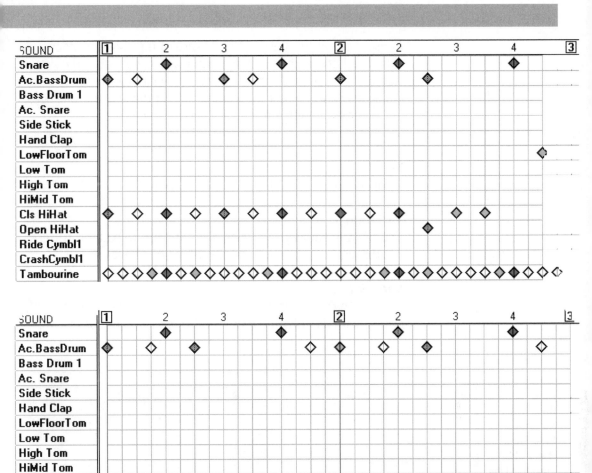

Rock ballad 2 (ROCKBAL2)

Conspicuous at the start by the absence of the hi hat or other
riding background beat. Snare drum plays on beats 2 and 4 with
closed hi hats playing steady eighths. Straight eighth note fills
would probably be best for a pattern going the way this one does,
but experiment with a few strategically placed syncopated
sixteenths.

Fill
An almost non eventful tom fill – but it works!

Variation 1
The ride cymbal playing straight eighths helps to pad this pattern
out through a chorus or middle 8 section of a song.

Variation 2
Same as the basic pattern but uses straight eighths on the ride
cymbal with a crash on the first beat of every other bar or two.

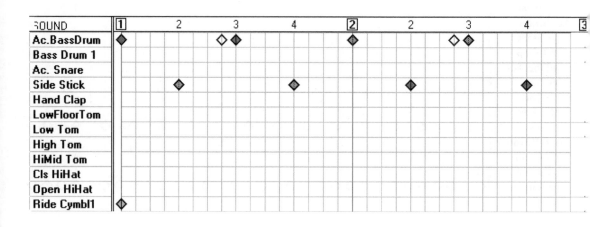

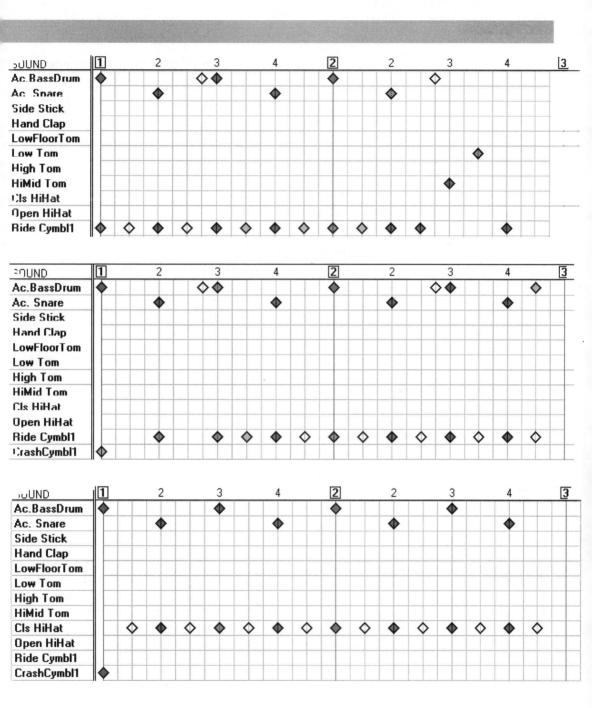

6   GM drum map

All files are mapped to the standard GM/GS/XG note assignments. They will sound correct across a wide variety of devices from most manufacturers, including Creative Labs, Yamaha, Roland, Korg, GEM and others.

All files are in format 1 (multitrack / multi-channel). Where MIDI controllers are used, they are as follows:

007 = Volume
010 = Panning
091 = Reverb send level (GM/GS only)
093 = Chorus send level (GM/GS only)
011 = Expression – used for crescendos and decrescendos*.

*   *Note* If your instrument does not respond to this controller then you must use your sequencer's edit facilities to convert controller 011 (expression) to controller 007 (volume).

To increase or decrease an instrument or part's pitch bend range, the following controllers are used:

101 = MSB 000
100 = LSB 000
006 = Data entry (use value two of this parameter to adjust the coarse pitch bend sensitivity.
101 = MSB 127
100 = LSB 127
Program change = sets the part or instrument to a particular 'voice' or 'timbre'.

There may be other controllers used which might be specific to XG or GS such as 000 and 032 preceding the program change event which may at times be used for bank select messages. If the sequences contain these controllers and you experience any difficulties, especially with older non-GM/GS equipment, delete these events and re-save the file (to a backup disk). Yamaha's new XG format uses MIDI control 000 set to 127 when turning a 'normal' part into a drum part.

GM drum/percussion map and program numbers/names as per GM/GS specification

The following is a list of drum/percussion map and the program change numbers used in the GM/GS specification. The DRM file on disk is for Cubase users who don't have a GM drum module or drum machine. Please refer to your software manual for info on how to install and use this DRM or drum map. If you need to remap the drum/percussion tracks to another standard try using either your sequencer's drum edit page, if it has one, or *logical edit*, as employed in Steinberg's Pro 24 and Cubase. It would be better if you can configure your module(s) to GM/GS and save all your setups via SysEx rather than having to edit each and every song file.

		Map for Standard set	Brush set	Orch. set			Map for Standard set	Brush set	Orch. set
D#0	27	High Q	Sound FX	Closed hat	B2	59	Ride cymbal 2		
E0	28	Slap	Sound FX	Pedal hat	C3	60	Hi bongo		
F0	29	Scratch push	Sound FX	Open hat	C#3	61	Lo bongo		
F#0	30	Scratch pull	Sound FX	Ride cymb	D3	62	Conga slap		
G0	31	Sticks			D#3	63	Conga hi		
G#0	32	Square click	Sound FX		E3	64	Conga lo		
A0	33	Metronome click	Sound FX		F3	65	Timbale hi		
A#0	34	Metronome bell	Sound FX		F#3	66	Timbale lo		
B0	35	Kick drum 2		Concert BD2	G3	67	Go go bell hi		
C1	36	Kick drum 1		Concert BD1*	G#3	68	Go go bell lo		
C#1	37	Sidestick			A3	69	Cabasa		
D1	38	Snare drum 1	Brush tap	Concert SD	A#3	70	Maracas		
D#1	39	Hand claps	Brush slap	Castanets	B3	71	Whistle short		
E1	40	Snare drum 2	Brush swirl	Concert SD	C4	72	Whistle long		
F1	41	Lo tom 2		Timpani F	C#4	73	Short guiro		
F#1	42	Closed hat		Timpani F#	D4	74	Long guiro		
G1	43	Lo tom 1		Timpani G	D#4	75	Claves		
G#1	44	Pedal hat		Timpani G#	E4	76	Hi woodblock		
A1	45	Mid tom 2		Timpani A	F4	77	Lo woodblock		
A#1	46	Open hat		Timpani A#	F#4	78	Mute quica		
B1	47	Mid tom		Timpani B	G4	79	Open quica		
C2	48	Hi tom 2		Timpani C	G#4	80	Mute triangle		
C#2	49	Crash cymbal		Timpani C#	A4	81	Open triangle		
D2	50	Hi tom 1		Timpani D	A#4	82	Shaker		
D#2	51	Ride cymbal		Timpani D#	B4	83	Sleighbells		
E2	52	Chinese cymbal		Timpani E	C5	84	Castanets		
F2	53	Ride bell		Timpani F	C#5	85	Mute surdo		
F#2	54	Tambourine			D5	86	Open surdo		
G2	55	Splash cymbal			D#5	87			
G#2	56	Cow bell			E5	88	Applause		
A2	57	Crash cymbal 2		Concert cymb2					
A#2	58	Quijada		Concert cymb1					

7 GM Program change numbers

The following are the program numbers/names as per the GM/GS specifications.

Capital tones

Program no.	Name	Program no.	Name	Program no.	Name
000	Piano 1	043	Contrabass	086	5th saw wave
001	Piano 2	044	Tremolo strings	087	Bass and lead
002	Piano 3	045	Pizzicato strings	088	Fantasia
003	Honky tonk	046	Harp	089	Warm pad
004	E. piano 1	047	Timpani	090	Polysynth
005	E. piano 2	048	Strings	091	Space voice
006	Harpsichord	049	Slo strings	092	Bowed glass
007	Clav	050	Synth strings 1	093	Metal pad
008	Celesta	051	Synth strings 2	094	Halo pad
009	Glockenspiel	052	Choir aahs	095	Sweep pad
010	Music box	053	Voice oohs	096	Ice rain
011	Vibraphone	054	Synth vox	097	Soundtrack
012	Marimba	055	Orchestra hit	098	Crystal
013	Xylophone	056	Trumpet	099	Atmosphere
014	Tubular bells	057	Trombone	100	Brightness
015	Santur	058	Tuba	101	Goblin
016	Organ 1	059	Muted trumpet	102	Echo drops
017	Organ 2	060	French horn	103	Star theme
018	Organ 3	061	Brass 1	104	Sitar
019	Church organ 1	062	Synth brass 1	105	Banjo
020	Reed organ	063	Synth brass 2	106	Shamisen
021	French accordion	064	Soprano sax	107	Koto
022	Harmonica	065	Alto sax	108	Kalimba
023	Bandneon	066	Tenor sax	109	Bagpipe
024	Nylon strung guitar	067	Baritone sax	110	Fiddle
025	Steel strung guitar	068	Oboe	111	Shanai
026	Jazz guitar	069	English horn	112	Tinkle bell
027	Clean guitar	070	Bassoon	113	Agogo
028	Muted guitar	071	Clarinet	114	Steel drums
029	Overdrive guitar	072	Piccolo	115	Woodblock
030	Distortion guitar	073	Flute	116	Taiko
031	Guitar harmonics	074	Recorder	117	Melo tom 1
032	Acoustic bass	075	Pan flute	118	Synth drum
033	Fingered bass	076	Bottle blow	119	Reverse cymbal
034	Picked bass	077	Shakuhachi	120	Guitar fret noise
035	Fretless bass	078	Whistle	121	Fl.Key click
036	Slap bass 1	079	Ocarina	122	Seashore
037	Slap bass 2	080	Square wave	123	Bird
038	Synth bass 1	081	Saw wave	124	Telephone 1
039	Synth bass 2	082	Synth calliope	125	Helicopter
040	Violin	083	Chiffer lead	126	Applause
041	Viola	084	Charang	127	Gun shot
042	Cello	085	Solo vox		

These are just some of the recordings that I have referred to during some of my drum programming tutorials. The list is by no means exhaustive, but it should point you in the right direction, especially if you want to delve further into technique.

- *Soul Sacrifice* by Santana on the *Santana* LP, CBS Records. Drummer – Mike Shrieve.
- *Soul Sacrifice* by Santana on the *Woodstock* LP, Catillion Records. Drummer – Mike Shrieve.
- *Head, Hands, & Feet* by Santana live on the *Moonflower* LP, CBS Records. Drummer – Graham Lear.
- For jazz/funk drumming, check out *Chameleon* by Herbie Hancock on the *Head Hunters* LP, CBS Records. Drummer – Harvey Mason.
- Some great 'anything goes' drumming, check out *I'm A Man* by Chicago on the *Chicago Transit Authority* LP, CBS Records. Drummer – Daniel Seraphine.
- *Aja* by Steely Dan on the *Aja* LP, ABC Records. Drummer – Steve Gadd.
- For sambas and other world rhythms, check out George Duke's *Brazilian Love Affair* LP on Epic Records. Drummer – Ricky Lawson.
- For Soul and Dance drumming, check out Chaka Khan's *I Feel For You* LP on Warner Bros. Records. Drummer – various real and programmed drums and percussion.
- For 7/4s and 5/4s and other esoteric styles, check out *Birds Of Fire* by the Mahavishnu Orchestra on CBS Records. Drummer – Billy Cobham.
- For some great classic rock drumming, check out the *Abbey Road* LP on Apple Records. Drummer – Ringo Starr.
- For rock/jazz drumming, check out *Brother To Brother* by Gino Vinalli on A&M Records. Drummer – Mark Craney.
- For jazz/funk/fusion, check out Weather Report's *Birdland* on the *Heavy Weather* LP on CBS Records. Drummer – Alex Acuna.
- For some serious funk/jazz drumming – you need look no further than any one of the many Tower Of Power LPs released over the past 15 to 20 years. Even the old stuff is streets ahead of some of the current dance/funk material.
- For Cuban, Jazz and Latin, check out the group *Irakere live at the Newport Jazz Festival* on CBS Records.
- For rock/fusion, check out Simon Phillips on Jeff Beck's *Space Boogie* (a must).
- Drummers to look out for are Buddy Rich, Buddy Miles, Maurice White of Earth, Wind and Fire, Steve Ferrone of Average White Band, Carl Palmer of Emerson Lake and Palmer, Jeff Porcarno of Toto, Bobby Columby of Blood Sweat and Tears, Stix Hooper of The Crusaders, the list could be a few pages but you'll get the idea. These guys will point you in many directions, each, with their own brand and flavour of style.
- Percussionists to look out for are Sheila Escovedo, Armando Peraza, Airto, Tito Puente, Ray Barretto, Mongo Santamaria, Orestes Vilato, Ray Cooper, Bill Summers of the Head Hunters, Paulinho DaCosta. As above, the list is huge.

We are indebted to all of the above musicians and the countless unmentioned who for many years have continued to supply a virtually unlimited wealth of inspiration.

Index

Heavenly Music MIDI Software

AWARD WINNING SOFTWARE FROM THE INVENTORS OF THE BUILDING BLOCK SOFTWARE BIZ!

Drum & Percussion Patterns	Dr. Beat, Afro Cuba, Break Beats, Rhythms Greatest Hits Vols 1 & 2 Beat n Bass Grooves - £14.99 ea
Groove Files & Other bits	Dr. Rave, Techno Files, RapTrax Hit Shot, Jungle Grooves, Arptron, Jazz Riffs,, Pearly Gates £14.99 e Bytes n Pieces £19.99
Jam Files	Ultimate Blues Vols 1 & 2 Jam Files Vols 1 & 2 £14.99 ea

NEW - AWE CDROM

Over 200 SoundFonts for Creative Labs AWE32/64/64 Gold including Synths, Basses, Guitars, Strings, Brass, Choirs, Drums, Percussion, Woodwinds, Keyboards, Sound FX PLUS hundreds of WAV files and Drum and percussion loops. The ULTIMATE AWE accessory at just £49.99 plus postage & handling.

PO Box 3175 Clacton, Essex CO15 2RP
E-mail: heavenly@ortiz.demon.co.uk
Web site at : http://www.ortiz.demon.co.uk

Please add £1.50 uk p&p / £3.00 world p&p
For CD products, add £3.60 uk, £6.60 world

For sequencer users!

Sequencer Secrets

**Over 150 power tips for
MIDI sequencer users**

Ian Waugh

108 pp ★ 216 x 138 mm ★ illustrated
ISBN 1870775 37 6

- 29 hands on projects
- Unlease the full potential of your sequencer
- Suitable for all software sequencers
- Become a power user
- Section on troubleshooting

£9.95
inc P&P

The manual may tell you how your sequencer works, but Sequencer Secrets goes beyond any manual. In this concise, creative and intensely practical book, Ian Waugh explains how you can get the best from any software sequencer. It contains a collection of hints and tips acquired over many years of experience with a wide range of software sequencers. It explains how to master functions you may have previously ignored, how to use short cuts to speed up your work, and how to turn your sequencer from a recording tool into a creative music machine.

The book will show you how to:

Optimise your MIDI system ★ Create MIDI echoes ★ Create instant harmonies ★ Humanise your drum patterns ★ Use controller messages more effectively ★ Use quantisation more effectively ★ Create more realistic instrument parts ★ Program gate effects ★ Use sequences live

A troubleshooting section helps you track down MIDI anomalies like double notes, volume dropouts, stuck notes and instruments going out of tune.

'Indispensable' *Future Music*
'Packed with helpful hints' *Sound on Sound*

Order hotline 01732 770893

PC Publishing
Tel 01732 770893 • Fax 01732 770268
email pcp@cix.compulink.co.uk
Website http://www.pc-pubs.demon.co.uk

Call our
order hotline
01732
770893

newtronic

Music production has undergone great change in the last few years. Music computing has opened the door to production for many aspiring musicians. Professionals have had the opportunity to rethink their production techniques resulting in the creation of many new musical genres such as the Dance explosion breaking both conventional ideas and borders. Newtronic is proud to be part of that global culture.

We have created a range of new products that aid the production process of music including up-to-date Dance styles such as Drum'n'Bass, House, Techno, Trance, Trip Hop, Rave and Dreamhouse. Our midifile loop & tool disks, sampling collections, midi software & midi books are the essence of a 7 year long successful track record in supplying tools for music programmers. Whether you are a professional or a hobbyist, using our products results in a new experience of **creative control & inspiration**.

When you make music, you want it to come out the way you hear it in your head. With the pro studio loops series we introduced a range of midifile disks which give you the freedom to choose, use or abuse the various grooves it contains. Make fresher, more creative, original, professional tracks. You can analyse the complex dance grooves of the Newtronic loop & tool disks and you have all the space you need to make them part of your sound. Each disk is style specific - you get what you ask for. If you are into dance music you can't afford not to talk to us.

newtronic ltd.

62B Manor Avenue
London SE4 1TE

Tel. +44 (0)181 691 1087
Fax +44 (0)181 691 2284

email sales@newtronic.com
online shop

www.newtronic.com

pro studio loops

house garage
breakbeat house
original jungle
intelligent drum'n'bass
funky classics
swingbeat breakbeat
dance percussion

pro studio tools

arpeggio kit
midi gates
filter kit
xg/gs wizard

construction kits

techno & dance kit
trip hop kit
trance kit
funk factory kit
dreamhouse kit
electronica & big beat kit

creative groove tools

dance, deep house + new movements
post-jungle & beyond

production libraries

club nation
hip hop nation
jungle nation
rave nation

pro studio elements

club bass
rave bass

midi busker disks

acoustic guitar vol.1
acoustic guitar vol.2
electric guitar
latin guitar
beat busker